# Bureaucracy in Action

# Bureaucracy in Action

Editors
I.C. Srivastava
B.D. Joshi

Published under the auspices of
**Management Development Academy, Jaipur**

**RAWAT PUBLICATIONS**
Jaipur • New Delhi • Bangalore • Hyderabad • Guwahati

ISBN 978-81-316-0525-7



*Published by*
Prem Rawat for **Rawat Publications**
Satyam Apts, Sector 3, Jawahar Nagar, Jaipur 302 004 (India)
Phone: 0141 265 1748/7006 Fax: 0141 265 1748
E-mail: info@rawatbooks.com
Website: www.rawatbooks.com

*New Delhi Office*
4858/24, Ansari Road, Daryaganj, New Delhi 110 002
Phone: 011 2326 3290

Also at *Bangalore, Hyderabad* and *Guwahati*

Typeset by Rawat Computers, Jaipur
Printed at Nice Printing Press, New Delhi

# Contents

## Part II
## Cherishable Memories



## Part III
## The Chief Ministers

# Acknowledgements

Publications have come out from time to time, which provide detailed account of the achievements of the members of Indian Administrative Service. No doubt, they are a source of inspiration for young officers. Therefore, it has been felt that we may also present, before them, some more such events which are unforgettable and cherishable and may remain fresh in their memory lane for years to come and may also be a guiding factor.

Since two major publications—*The Collectors Recollect,* edited by Late Shri Mohan Mukerji and Professor Ramesh K. Arora, and *In the Corridors of Power*, edited by Professor Ramesh K. Arora—had some chapters of similar nature, we were tempted to include some of them in this book. We are highly grateful to Professor Arora who not only gave his consent but also guided us at various stages of publication and also devoted much of his valuable time in facilitating its publication.

We are also indebted to the eminent contributors who found time to pen down their papers and for this purpose they had to go deep in their past to recollect and provide detailed account of those events.

We are thankful to the staff of Management and Development Academy, Jaipur, specially Shri Virendra Mehta and Ms Shree Priya who helped us in shaping this book. We are also highly thankful to Rawat Publications, Jaipur, for publishing this book with assiduity.

# 1

# Introduction

## Looking Back on Civil Service

**I.C. Srivastava and B.D. Joshi**

In a developing country like India, dynamics of public administration demand and call forth fast changing and adaptive responses to challenges and problems faced by civil servants in dealing with day-to-day and long-term administrative matters. The very fact that IAS, the successor civil service to ICS, has not only survived the trials and tribulations of the partition of the country but also provided a firm foundation for all round development is a tribute to the vision and wisdom of the founding fathers of our Constitution including Sardar Patel, the first Home Minister of India. It was Patel who gave the first clarion call to IAS officers 'to maintain to the utmost the impartiality and incorruptibility of administration' by keeping away from 'politics' and 'communal wrangles' and 'render your service without fear or favour and without any expectations of extraneous rewards'.

Sixty years of India's experience in development and experiment in democracy has brought forth the fact that IAS, the generalist service, has been par excellence in patches of periods and specific situations especially, e.g., in delivering general elections, decadal census and calamity-relief besides fighting wars, mainly against Pakistan. Besides, its 'omnipresence', though eroded by inroads of other services, has stood ground but its so-called 'omnipotence' is a factum of past. However, time and again individual civil servants have not only risen to the occasion in demanding, gruelling tasks but also left an imprint, by their qualities of head and heart, on the administrative set-up or locale especially their district collectorates. They are still fondly remembered by those who had seen them at work and faintly by others who have merely heard of them.

Keeping these perspectives and historic imperatives and legacies of administration of Rajasthan, we have cajoled and persuaded some of our senior colleagues (though retired from service but not tired of doing some social good) who could look back on their work and contribution to the district or in assignment where they gathered significant learning experience, which could benefit posterity of civil servants.

Therefore, with a view to enriching and enlivening our efforts, we have complied this book in three parts: the first devoted to 'unforgettables'—events, episodes and kernels of experience, the second dedicated to 'cherishables', i.e., veterans and stalwarts among administrators whose rich memories we cherish and would like to share in writing with our present and future generations of civil servants and, in the third part, authors have narrated their recollections about the Chief Ministers with whom they came in close contact.

While this book does not claim to be representative of decades of experience of 'intricate and delicate tasks' performed in multifarious roles by the IAS, we have made an earnest effort to give space to our earliest administrators in post-independence period and thereafter to others who have responded to our call and request to contribute to this book. We do hope that this book will not only be found interesting and informative about the times gone by but also serve as a reference and research material for those who seek to explore, analyse and feel inspired to write their own memoirs in a historic perspective.

Rajasthan, the erstwhile Rajputana which was a conglomerate of 21 states, has made a near smooth transition from a feudal society and set-up of administration to the modern, now technology-driven also, administrative structure of regulatory and developmental administration largely due to the sagacity and capabilities of civil servants backed by wise and visionary political leaders such as

M.L. Sukhadia and B.S. Shekhawat, who have made an immense contribution to modern Rajasthan and its development.

Though self-centric in experience, the contributions made in this book do exemplify the nature of law and order and other problems and some of them may serve as basis for case studies for training of probationers in training academies and institutes.

Finally, the knowledge, experience and appreciation of unforgettable events and cherishable personalities may also open up avenues for further administrative reforms for the challenge before administration still remains as to how to make public service management effective and also formulate more open, transparent and accountable systems of delivery of public services in a professional manner. In negotiating and facing the cataclysmic changes and challenges, a twenty-first century young administrator may seek solace and silent reprieve in browsing through the various ways and approaches that enabled the civil servants, in past half a century, to overcome administrative problems.

### A Testing Predicament

In his paper, 'A Testing Predicament', J.S. Mehta has narrated a detailed account of the critical situation he had to face when he was Collector, Chittorgarh in the year 1948. He had gone to Deogarh to take possession of a tehsil building, which was earlier in the control and possession of jagirdars and then declared as state property. He was confident of the cooperation of Deogarh Raoji, an ex-jagirdar, with whom he also had family relations. But the dual role played by Raoji created a very critical situation, and he had to face a violent mob. How tactfully he handled this grave situation gives a very interesting account and a lesson for those who come across such situations.

### Mythological Rudder Collapsed

'All is well that ends well' is a truism that holds good both in personal life and in administrative career check posts which an officer carves and charts for himself. In the same vein, therefore, Pradyumna Kumar narrates another law and order episode about his initial years in service as a Magistrate in Jalore district which is a desert district still lagging behind in women's literacy and other socio-economic indicators. No wonder, fifty years ago, Purohit community sought exemption from payment of land revenue based on the sheet anchor of their superstitious belief that their ancestors had not paid any revenue even in mythological times of Raja Hiranyakashyap. This firm belief or 'mythological rudder' as the author terms it had prompted a middle-aged believer to pierce his abdomen two inches deep by an 18-inch-long dagger. This 'unforgettable sight' of a man lying in a tent on a mattress with a 13-year-old daughter sitting by his side and blood clots and stains spluttered over his body created a unique and somewhat historic situation for Shri Kumar to deal with. By sympathizing with him, he could record his narration of entire sequence of events including 'Tarkhad' ceremony in the temple of their community deity in Kalindari village, wherein he had taken a vow before piercing his abdomen with the dagger, which no one was allowed to extricate from his body lest it desanctified his vow.

Telephone lines having been rendered unserviceable, the communication with Collector was possible only through two railway station masters of Bagra and Bhinmal. But before Collector could return to tackle the situation, rain god helped Kumar and the police force led by District SP. The fury of rain created a chaos and forced the protesters to run helter-skelter leaving behind the Tarkhad ceremony hero-protester only to be first treated by a doctor on the spot and thereafter shifted to the District Hospital at night, to the great relief of all, including the Purohit protesters.

This bizarre and unique incident only illustrates the range and scope of law and order situations faced by successive administrative officers in Rajasthan.

## Generating Faith and Goodwill

It is almost proverbial that IAS officers, in line with ICS fraternity, generally look back with nostalgia to their district assignment and cull rich and positive experiences to be put down in reminiscences. V.B.L. Mathur, however, is an exception to this practice, if not the rule and proves it to the hilt. His experience as the Registrar, Cooperative Societies on deputation to Himachal Pradesh, was no less exciting and satisfying in a fulfilling task undertaken by him to secure remunerative price to the seed potato growers by fighting against traders and middlemen besides overcoming imponderables and hurdles in accomplishing a seemingly Herculean task in the given circumstances.

Mathur set about his new duties by holding long-drawn meetings with field and headquarters officers besides undertaking extensive tours of the potato growing areas; he met large number of farmers and took his team officers into confidence. He sent selected ones to Maharashtra to study the market and negotiate with Apex Marketing Federation to take bulk supplies. All this was done with a well thought out strategy which also included looking after the officers from Maharashtra and persuading even Chief Secretary to go on tour with him so as to involve transport and other departments in this venture to bring succour and prosperity to the best variety potato growers who were earlier totally dependent on traders and *arahatiyas* and with whom they had to leave behind their stocks to be sold at latter's will for their own huge profit.

Mathur's sympathy with farmers, his faith in the cooperative system of governance and confidence in his team to deliver certainly paid off. In the first year itself, the farmers received 200 per cent price over what they had been earlier paid. Federation's prices announced on All India Radio brought about the necessary transparency.

No wonder, Mathur's vision, wisdom and sagacity won him all round admiration and praise. Farmers developed such affection for him that they kept writing to him and visiting him for many years to come in acknowledgement of his bold initiative and action to bring prosperity to their families. What a greatly satisfying and self-fulfilling task indeed it was and a matter of envy and emulation too, for many officers.

## Threatened Confrontation Averted

A close contemporary, in civil service, of Pradyumna Kumar, Sudhindra Gemawat has refreshingly recalled his role as Sub-Divisional Magistrate and early stirrings of caste rivalry and brewing conflict between Rajputs and Jat peasantry. Rajputs had ruled in various states of Rajputana and tormented Jat peasantry by extracting land revenue and other customary tributes as jagirdars and chieftains in the erstwhile Rajputana. With the advent of democracy, election results based on majority had turned tables and Jat leaders dominated the state scenario as ministers and MLAs. Rajputs too had their strongholds but were outnumbered in most areas. Against this backdrop, Gemawat has refreshed his memory and narrated the threatening law and order situation when Nathu Ram Mirdha, the pre-eminent Jat leader and minister in M.L. Sukhadia's cabinet was to address, at village Thob of Balotra Subdivision, a public meeting of Kisans for which farmers had gathered in large numbers. But Mirdha had made some derogatory remarks against Rajputs in a meeting held earlier at Samdari village of Barmer district, which was also a part of Balotra Subdivision. Minister Mirdha cleverly advised Gemawat to deal with Rajputs by his discretion and judgement. The dilemma of a young officer in dealing with Rajputs gathered in large numbers, with the backing of eight police personnel was understandable. However, he allowed them to join the public meeting wherein the Minister, sagacious as he was, softened his tone and addressed them all in a conciliatory manner averting a confrontational caste-conflict situation. Gemawat's faith in God almighty also helped him a lot.

## Yes, I Recall

Law and order, being the primary responsibility of an IAS officer in the initial years, may be a decade in most cases, the contributors have nostalgically recalled their varied experiences in situations that not only tested their mettle but also exposed their personal qualities of head and heart, thus enabling them to 'sail through' with a bit of luck or chance factor and 'God overhead'. To begin with, Pradyumna Kumar has 'delved deep into the treasure trove' (to borrow his own phrase) of his memory to present to us a near 'photostat' of his experience as a trainee officer about the first Panchayat elections in Rajasthan held early in 1960. It is amazing and sounds strange but true that a local Panchayat-level candidate had started nursing suspicion, at that point in time, that administrative machinery was capable of manipulating polls in favour of or against a candidate. His suspicion was grounded in the fact that the opposing candidate had suggested and helped in securing alternative safe accommodation for the polling party. The exemplary conduct of Kumar and his team not only set the record straight but also compelled the disgruntled candidate to remark that 'polls were impartial and satisfying'. Shri Kumar learnt his first objective lesson in a volatile situation in which police force had arrived to back him only at the time of declaration of results, wherein by a sheer stroke of luck a Central Excise and Customs party head passing that way had communicated his requirement of police force to the concerned officers in time.

### Stern Action with a Smile

V.D. Sharma had to face a different situation when he was Collector, Jaipur, in the year 1967, and had to arrest some influential political leaders of the opposition parties, which included leaders such as Shri Bhairon Singh Shekhawat, Master Adityendra, Satish Chandra Agarwal, Hari Krishna Vyas, Kumbharam Arya and Ramkaran Joshi and put them in jail for breach of prohibitory orders. A problem had arisen when the state government took a decision to release them and these leaders refused to leave the jail premises. How tactfully Shri Sharma handled this situation by forcing them to leave the jail premises and still kept them in good humour is a lesson to learn as such situations are quite frequent these days.

### The Deluge Dilemma and an Unenviable Election Night

I.C. Srivastava has recapitulated two memorable events of his tenure as SDO Bharatpur (1968–1970), namely, the unprecedented floods in Gambhiri river filling Ajan bund to its brim, thus endangering the Ghana Bird Sanctuary and Bharatpur town and its people on one hand and the conduct of election at a polling station throughout the night, thus averting an imminent law and order situation—a unique experience in itself.

### Fighting the Flames and Visit to Parbat Ali

In I.C. Srivastava's narrative, a detailed account has been given of his efforts which he had to make, to maintain peace and bring normalcy during Indo-Pak War in the year 1971. As Collector and District Magistrate of Barmer, it was a highly challenging job. When there were many air assaults by Pak Air Force and continuous threat to life and property of the citizens, he had to coordinate between army authorities and police and also to keep up the morale of citizens. He had come across many critical situations such as bombing and burning of Railway godowns and huge damage of property but the way citizens helped District Administration whole-heartedly with high spirits are really unforgettable events and an inspiration for administrators.

His visit to the Pakistan's area which was occupied by Indian Army during that period, along with Major General R.D.R. Anand gave such thrilling moments to his team that are difficult to forget.

## An Unexpected Encounter

In another paper 'An Unexpected Encounter', he has given a detailed account about his meeting with an ex-dacoit Thakur Balwant Singh. It was in March 1972, when he was Collector and District Magistrate, Barmer, he had gone for inspection of Police Station, Bakhasar. On reaching Bakhasar Police Station, this unexpected encounter took place. Thakur Balwant Singh came out of the arched courtyard of the police station and greeted him with words 'Khamma Ghani' and Rajput's chivalrous slight bow paying his respects to the institution of the District Head. Thakur Balwant Singh, an ex-dacoit, was earlier a terror across desert areas and had surrendered before Rajasthan Government after 1965 Indo-Pak War. In this paper, he has also narrated how he was able to avoid his prospective dinner with Thakur Balwant Singh. He has drawn an interesting account of the colourful personality of Thakur, and the image of his bedecked horse is still fresh in his mind.

## Guarding the Gardens

What an apt title to a yeoman service rendered by an 'old guard' of state administration! P.K.B. Kurup recollects how 'a picture of devastation came before me' and the orders (auction of 18 gardens in the district) I was asked to sign appeared to me to be a death warrant, within a fortnight of his assuming charge. Next morning, driving through three to four gardens before going to office, enchanting 'sylvan setting' cast its spell on him. After consulting users of gardens and officers of the district, who were also made to inspect the gardens, a consensus emerged that the gardens should be saved and managed better. As Collector of Alwar district, Shri Kurup sent a detailed report to Chief Secretary proposing that most of the gardens should be retained and transferred to various departments and the remaining few could be auctioned.

The matter went up to the Finance Minister and the Chief Minister who not only appreciated the stand taken by district administration but also readily approved its recommendations.

This eco-friendly approach and decisive action on the part of district administration not only saved the gardens for posterity, thus enabling succeeding generations to enjoy their environs but has also proved to be an objective lesson in that government can ill afford to let down district administration where sheer public interest is involved and embedded and perceived as such by public at large.

## VVIP Visits Redefined

Mohan Mukerji was one of the most accomplished and well-known personalities in Rajasthan's public administration. An amiable and pleasant person, he exuded and inspired confidence in colleagues and subordinates in all assignments that came his way. Needless to add, he retained his charm and amiability even in the midst of onerous duties as Chief Secretary.

In this extract from his book, *Non-story of a Chief Secretary During Emergency Et Cetra*, he reminisces about some VVIP visits during his stint as Chief Secretary (1975–1977). Among VVIPS he has included Runa Laila, the well-known singer from Bangladesh, by redefining the term VVIP to mean 'any outstanding personality who draws crowds which require some form of control'. Runa was a craze among all sections of listeners—old and young—in three countries across the subcontinent and was, therefore, a roaring success at Jaipur by her vivacious performance and singing of Urdu, Hindi and Sindhi songs.

During political VVIPs' visits, the state administration is fully geared to make all arrangements, including meticulously planned protocol matters of state reception, send-off and banquet, under the guidance and leadership of Chief Secretary. During Mukerji's tenure, the state hosted a number of VVIPs who included President, Vice President, Prime Minister and Central Ministers. He fondly recalls the visit of President Fakhruddin Ali Ahmed when the Housing Board shopping complex was inaugurated by him in the new and large colony of Jawahar Nagar, Jaipur, but still under construction, besides a visit to kachchi basti. The then Collector of Jaipur, to quote Mukerji, 'a colourful personality, spoke in very high-flown Hindi which went over the head of many persons including myself and perhaps the President'.

Prime Minister Indira Gandhi's visit to Bharatpur, Udaipur and Ajmer was the most important and exacted hardest work, from all those associated with it. Even a slight failure would have caused a great embarrassment but thanks to detailed planning by a mastermind like Mukerji, who put in all his acumen and energy, made the visit a success as it was.

Civil service neutrality and anonymity come into play in a great measure during such VVIP visits especially in a case such as Sanjay Gandhi's visit. As PM's son and popular Youth Congress leader, he drew large crowds. Both Chief Secretary and IG Police were present but 'at a discreet distance since the functions were not organised by the State Government as such we had to be near enough to take decisions'. They heaved a sign of relief after the visit passed off without any untoward incident.

His reminiscences in two books authored by him will be of lasting value to students and practitioners of public administrators.

### Agonising Situation Ended Well

In her paper, Krishna Bhatnagar has given a detailed account how she had to face a strange situation as Collector and District Magistrate, Ajmer. It happened when a supposedly non-violent elephant, accompanying the entourage of Sadhus, created a havoc in the town of Ajmer and the district administration had to handle this unprecedented situation. It is a very interesting account and depicts how an agonising situation ultimately turned out as smooth affair.

### Disaster Management

A paper relating to flood by R.S. Kumat narrates the details: how this situation was handled with no loss to human life and minimum damage to property. It was during his tenure as Collector of Ajmer in the year 1976, when he was extremely busy in managing the Urs Fair which is organised every year in the memory of Sufi Khwaja Moinuddin Chishti. On this occasion, Ajmer attracts huge gathering, and lakh of people assemble for 8–10 days. Due to heavy rainfall, most of the areas were submerged with water and it was extremely difficult to manage the affairs in such circumstances. Disaster management is one of the toughest jobs of administrators, and this paper shows how this can also be smoothly managed with patience, perseverance and tactfulness.

### A Tale of Herculean Effort

During the period of Emergency, I.S. Kavadia's posting as Collector of Kota district brought a windfall of freedom to thousands of tribals not only from bondage of exploiters in terms of long years of labour but also redeemed their debts in thousands of cases under the dispensation of Rajasthan Scheduled Debtors (Moratorium of Debt) and Liquidation of Debt Acts of 1976. Besides, land alienated by them largely by unregistered and unrecorded mortgage and sale deeds were restored to them by an Herculean and heroic effort made by Kavadia and his team of officers in district administration.

Of course, the newly promulgated legislation as aforesaid and the then amended provisions of Rajasthan Tenancy Act (RTA) 1955, especially Sec. 43 providing imprisonment up to one year in cases of unlawful possession of land after the satisfaction of mortgage or deed, proved the most potent and effective weapon in the multi-pronged strategy and armoury of measures enforced by a determined, single-minded and concerted approach adopted by Kavadia.

It may be recalled that the institution of Collector, highly respected otherwise, was held in awe by people in general and proved terrifying to the core for criminals during the heydays of Emergency (1975–1976) when Kavadia was posted as Collector, Kota. Even so, he undertook such extensive tours into the interior and forested areas of Shahabad Tehsil that this personal contact brought him face to face with misery and utter ignorance arising from near total illiteracy and poverty among the tribals. Tears welled up in his eyes during his first encounter with a gathering of tribals. Thus, unfolded their saga of freedom, and altogether nearly 31,000 tribals benefited from various measures—freedom from bondage of labour and debt and restoration of land in a short period of one year. It was, however, a different story as to how many of those tribals could retain their land and freedom after Emergency was over in 1977 and in years thereafter.

### Commitment Brings Success

I.C. Srivastava has given an interesting account of events during the period he was Collector and District Magistrate, Sri Ganganagar, during 1976–1977. One event relates to the family planning drive during the period of Emergency, when in a period of four days nearly 2,500 persons were operated upon and it was due to dedicated efforts of doctors who put their heart and soul in their work. The local support and cooperation and huge response received can never be wiped out from memory. Another event relates to the allotment of surplus land resumed under the urban ceiling laws, to landless persons on a huge scale. It was done so swiftly and with such a zeal by five young IAS officers that it is still fresh in his mind.

### Determination and Commitment Brought Justice

Abhimanyu Singh as Collector and District Magistrate, Tonk, has narrated how firm determination and commitment for a cause can bring justice to those who had been deprived of their land by influential persons. He had to fight hard at different levels and even approached Revenue Minister to explain how poor and deprived persons belonging to Scheduled Caste were victims of the exploiters. Ultimately, this battle was won, and weaker sections of the society could get justice.

### Rebuilding RIPA

H.C. Mathur Institute of Public Administration, Jaipur (HCM RIPA), also colloquially called OTS, was formally christened as such after the historic floods of the 19th July 1981, which broke record of 150 years in Jaipur. The original OTS building and the campus suffered the most in the havoc caused by the floods, which had destroyed hundreds of houses in kachchi bastis of Jaipur. Fortunately, immediately after the floods, it was headed by an IAS officer of the calibre and mettle of M.L. Mehta, Secretary to Chief Minister in earlier Janata Party Government, who rose to be Chief Secretary later.

Crisis draws out the best in an officer's personality as he puts into use all his resources of imagination, creativity, teamwork, grit and determination. Mehta amply demonstrated all this and much more. The campus community rose as one man from 'depth of despair', and then their teamwork helped salvage whatever they could from the wreckage including 25,000 books. Gradually, essential services were restored after marooned campus community had 'passed through "hell" without any water, power or milk supply'.

Joining the institute on the 13th August 1981, the initial breakthrough or kick-start was provided by his decision to restart the training programmes on the 31st August 1981. The crisis provided an opportunity to revamp the systems and build afresh with innovative approaches. Training programmes recommenced in Shamiyanas put up in front of hostel. The trainers, the staff and faculty all faced and shared the tribulations.

The road link was restored with great difficulties in November 1981. But 'the ravines formed around the building were too dangerous to be left alone', as Mehta remarks. They were filled up, and in the final phase a beautiful forest park came up after years of planning and hard work. The new building came up in record time with constant care and interaction of the Director with architect and his team. In the next phase, training facilities were upgraded and 'regionalised' at Udaipur, Kota, Jodhpur and Bikaner. Training moved to new frontiers and systems were improved immensely.

In retrospect, Mehta derived great satisfaction from this memorable experience; so will the readers gain after going through the rebuilding of this premier training institute of the country, which has, over the years, continued to host a number of national and international conferences as well.

## Price of Uprightness

In the other administrative episode, Rajendra Bhanawat has highlighted how even small-time politicians such as a Pradhan of Panchayat Samiti can play havoc with procedure and fair play and get away too with the support of powers that be when public interest is thrown to winds despite best efforts made by upright officers. As Chief Executive Officer, Zila Parishad of Bhilwara district, Bhanawat tried to enforce the guidelines of the state government by seeking to appoint candidates as teachers in various Panchayat Samitis (based on the recommendations of DEC [District Establishment Committee] headed by Zila Pramukh). But he ultimately failed to accomplish his task as CEO Zila Parishad in case of PS Shahpura as Pradhan (who had several criminal cases registered against him) wanted to retain, in service, ad-hoc teachers appointed by him earlier in the absence of selected ones. In fact, he was able to manage convening of a special meeting of Zila Parishad in which a decision was taken to retain the ad-hoc teachers in addition to newly appointed candidates, thus increasing the total strength by 27 posts against the likely sanction of 20 posts in 10 schools. Earlier, BDO was suspended by the Collector for acting under pressure to reverse his own order, thus retaining ad-hoc teachers in place of new appointees. His charge was handed over to Tehsildar who again reversed BDO's order, thus creating a piquant situation for the Pradhan, who manipulated the Zila Parishad meeting cited above. Surprisingly, Collector also became a party to this decision. No wonder, he remained a mute spectator even after orders of transferring Shri Bhanawat from Bhilwara were received.

Transfer is no punishment as an administrative cliché goes. But the morale of an officer with rectitude is too small a stake, at times, even for superior officers when politicians rule the roost and make hay while the sun shines. Who listens? For the masters lack the will to be righteous and would continue to do so in a foreseeable future.

### Family Planning Camp Tragedy

In another episode, Gemawat recreates, for us, the scenario of a family planning camp as it was then called. A rural woman had apparently died of reaction from an injection before being operated. As District Magistrate Sikar, he tackled this potential law and order problem in the only manner it was possible by shifting the body from Ajeetgarh village to Government District Hospital apparently for treatment, after which she was declared dead by the senior doctors. As no medical negligence was obvious, no action was called for against the operating doctors who had administered the same injection to all other women before operation and no reaction was reported in any case. As in life, in administration too 'all is well that ends well', of course, in this case only for doctors and district administration officers. The family and seven kids had lost their beloved mother.

### Firmness and Quick Decisions Bring Good Results

B.D. Joshi has brought out the unpredictability and potential of grave communal conflict arising from small law and order incidents—the first one occurred in Gangapur of Sawai Madhopur district, resulting from the death of a student of Meena community due to the injury caused and other event by throwing of 'Gulal on Holi' by a Mohammedan student and the others in Pisangan of Ajmer district.

His chance arrival in Gangapur on way to Nadauti enabled him to mobilise resources, including requisitioning of PAC from Agra, UP, by engaging the crowd into negotiation for compensation. A District Magistrate has to face such situations by not only mustering up courage and conviction in his line of action but also by summoning up all his resources of imagination, skill in patient negotiation and above all faith in God. This event reveals all this.

The situation at Pisangan in Ajmer was nipped in the bud by timely imposition of Section 144 Cr PC prohibitory orders and arrest of a few persons involved in the incident. But Shri Joshi had the courage of conviction in making a request to the Chief Minister to instruct the local minister not to visit Pisangan in the tense situation. This further defused the situation and brought peace and normalcy.

In Sikar district of which he was asked to take charge immediately in the aftermath of Deorala Sati incident, Joshi adopted other administrative measures namely by holding meeting of representatives of all political parties and senior officers of the district to chalk out line of action. He could seek such wholehearted cooperation that even Deorala village residents decided to prevent further glorification of Sati by setting up local committees in support of Sec. 144 Cr PC order promulgated by the administration.

Shri Joshi could also enlist support of all sections of people in fighting famine and extending relief to poor rural people. Balram Jakhar, the then MP for Lok Sabha, and Ram Deo Singh, a local minister, extended their cooperation and guidance to administration especially for arranging free fodder from Punjab.

District administration does deliver services and relief in trying circumstances, and this is precisely the reason why the institutions of Collector and District SP, the British legacy, have survived in post-indcpcndcncc pcriod.

### Jaipur Riots of 1990

In his paper, which relates to the riots in Jaipur in the year 1990, I.C. Srivastava has narrated the chain of events that led to the communal riot. As Divisional Commissioner, Jaipur, he had to coordinate with the local Army Officers for having a quick flag march in the city, which helped to ease the tense situation. He also coordinated with the district administration in such a way that it was possible to bring normalcy without much loss of time.

## Election Impasse: Churu District

Jagat Pal Singh has narrated an incident relating to State Assembly Elections in the year 1993, when he had to face a peculiar situation as District Magistrate, Churu. As District Election Officer, he had authorised certain persons as counting agents to watch the interest of the candidates who had nominated them. Thereafter, he got instructions from Commissioner, Bikaner Division, to withdraw the passes of those counting agents who were representing regional political parties. Probably, Commissioner was apprehensive of some problems due to these authorisations as per experience in Bikaner district. Shri Singh had no such problem in his district and cancellation of the passes of counting agents would have created more problems. Though he explained this situation to the Commissioner, Bikaner Division, she was insisting for the cancellation and also brought the matter to the notice of Chief Secretary. How this problem was ultimately solved and election process was completed smoothly is an interesting account and shows the confidence of the District Magistrate in assessing the situation and taking a firm stand.

## Mautana: Unwarranted Death Compensation Denied

Rajendra Bhanawat, a serving IAS officer, has done a yeoman service to tribal society especially of Dungarpur district where he was posted as Collector and District Magistrate in 1995. 'Mautana', the superstitious practice, in tribal society, of extracting compensation from the family or house in front of which a person had breathed his last for whatever reason, is the focus of this real-life tragic story which had the simmering potential of a more tragic law and order situation.

The payment of 'Mautana' had impoverished the poor persons who were, many times, forced to mortgage their property and sell jewellery as well even though a person had met with an accident and died of the same, such as in this episode narrated by Bhanawat himself. The body of Sarpanch Ramlal who had met with an accident by his own scooter and died at Ahmedabad after treatment by doctors was placed in front of Upsarpanch's house and kept there until intervention by District Magistrate Shri Bhanawat who held several rounds of meetings with tribals and Patidars. Upsarpanch belonged to the latter. The family members of late Ramlal, though sensible, felt themselves bound by Maulana superstition. Somehow, the demand of compensation was raised to ₹ 51 lakh, even though there was no evidence to connect Upsarpanch or his family with the accident. But this issue, somehow, also became a tribal versus non-tribal affair.

Thousands of tribals had gathered on call of customary drum beat and stored grains were put to fire. Lathi charge and tear gas shells fired by the police were of no avail and, therefore, police had to resort to firing, resulting in injury of three persons. Luckily for the administration, the crowd dispersed immediately and the injured were shifted first to Dungarpur and thereafter to Udaipur after transfusing blood to a seriously injured person, which was timely arranged by Bhanawat's wife.

Meanwhile, politicians including a Minister alongwith Divisional Commissioner, Udaipur, and IG from Jaipur who had arrived at Dungarpur were persuaded to convince the family of the deceased to accept the body and cremate the same. After a long-drawn dialogue, the family received the body at Vikasnagar village and cremated the same around midnight.

No doubt, Bhanawat displayed an exemplary administrative leadership in a volatile and tragic situation, even though parliamentary elections were only a fortnight away. Truly, it is an unforgettable incident full of many lessons for trainees as well as practising administrators, social workers and public at large.

## Cherishable Memories

In the second part of this book, memories have been recollected regarding some of the stalwarts of IAS of Rajasthan cadre who are no more on the scene but their contribution in the development of Rajasthan besides guidance and inspiration provided to the other members of service can never be forgotten. Three of them—S.L. Khurana, Mohan Mukerji and G.K. Bhanot—had been the Chief Secretary in the Government of Rajasthan while Yatindra Singh was Secretary, Finance, and also held other key posts in the government. Reminiscences about them speak volumes about qualities and virtues they possessed and reveal how they shaped the administration in their own way.

## The Chief Ministers

In the third part of this book, authors of the papers have given their impressions about the former Chief Ministers with whom they came in close contact. I.C. Srivastava has narrated his impressions about Mohan Lal Sukhadia, Barkatullah Khan and Bhairon Singh Shekhawat, who are no more on the scene but were all great persons who shaped the destiny of the state in their own way. Mohan Lal Sukhadia had been the Chief Minister of the state for seventeen years and is considered an architect of modern Rajasthan. His benevolent nature and complete grip over the administration was such a quality that won the hearts of the people. The author has cited some instances that reflect the magnanimity of Sukhadiaji. He has also recalled a few incidents about late Shri Barkatullah Khan, which reveal the essential human and humane side of his personality. His warmth and graceful behaviour touched everybody who came in his contact. Regarding B.S. Shekhawat who was also a self-made man, he has specially mentioned his humility, patience, perseverance and persuasive skill. Shekhawat who had complete command over administration, was a great judge of persons. These were the qualities that ultimately led him to a very high position of as Vice President of India.

P.N. Bhandari, in his recollection, has narrated his impressions about four ex-Chief Ministers, which include Shri Mohan Lal Sukhadia, Shri Haridev Joshi, Shri Shiv Charan Mathur and Shri B.S. Shekhawat. He has rightly mentioned that Shri Sukhadia was man of the masses and a great statesman. In respect of Shri Haridev Joshi under whom he had served in various capacities, he has specially appreciated his ability to take quick decisions besides his remarkable time management. Shri Joshi was man of few words, which carried great weight. Regarding Shri Shiv Charan Mathur, he is of the view that he was flexible enough and equally receptive to the contrary views expressed before him. He had a democratic approach and always gave patient hearing to others. He had also an opportunity to serve under Shri B.S. Shekhawat who was very witty and in his presence, one could not have tension. He was easily accessible to the people and officers. Shri Shekhawat was also democratic to the core and never displayed any authoritarian touch in his working as Chief Minister. He was very graceful and a good judge of persons.

# Part I

## Unforgettable Events

# 2

# A Testing Predicament

J.S. Mehta

In the princely state of Mewar, I was promoted to the post of District Collector and posted at Chittorgarh in 1947. I was a youth of about 26 years. It was merely a matter of chance that I had to devote a major part of my time and energy in doing social service rather than exercising administrative authority. As elsewhere, we also faced the refugee problem. Thousands of refugees coming from Sindh and Punjab could be seen at the railway station. I observed their plight, I talked to them, I felt one with them and I strongly felt that for the time being I was needed more among them than in the office.

### From Chittorgarh to Rajsamand

I considered refugees as my guests. If guests feel any inconvenience and if they do not feel properly attended to, it is a matter of disgrace to the host. And I, as Collector of Chittorgarh district, was the host. This feeling led me to move around the town and villages and among people for mobilising volunteers and collecting money and material. I spent a number of sleepless nights moving in trucks (as no other vehicles were available at that time), planning, reviewing, attending to the refugees personally and supervising the work. I was working with vigour and enthusiasm. I felt no fatigue. Conversely, I felt satisfaction and joy in rendering the essential services to my fellow human beings. I had not become conscious of the fact that the refugee problem had dominated my head and heart till I received the orders of my transfer to Rajsamand.

At that time, I did not imagine, nor probably did the government, that the most challenging task as part of my regulatory role was waiting for me in Rajsamand district. This happened when the government announced the abolition of the jagirs with effect from 1 February 1948. A gazette notification issued by the government said that all revenue powers vested so far in the jagirdars had ceased and the subordinates working with the jagirdars might continue to work as government employees. They were to hand over charge as employees of the jagirdars and to take over immediately as government officials. The change over was done smoothly in all the jagirs.

## The Mysterious Message

The year (1948) experienced famine-like conditions. A meagre amount of ₹ 50,000 was put at my disposal for conducting relief operations. In this connection, I, along with an Assistant Engineer, PWD, visited Deogarh, a tehsil headquarters situated among hills and valleys in the heart of dark woods. The Collector at that time did not have the facilities that are available today. He did not even have a vehicle at his disposal. I reached Deogarh by train, and the revenue officer of the Deogarh *thikana* was at the station to receive us. I was given to understand that at Deogarh some sort of vehicle would be made available by the Deogarh Raoji, the jagirdar of the area, to facilitate the performance of my duty. Instead, I received a message from him that I should not move out of the station as there was a Holi procession in the village, and it would not be advisable for me to get exposed to the public as they were not in their normal mood. He sent a message that he himself would come with a vehicle to conduct me to the places where relief work could be started and later he would take me to his guest house. I did not smell any conspiracy, nor was there any source or means of communication to verify the intention of Raoji. Moreover, our families were known to each other and had courteous relations. I had to rely on Raoji's words. Soon, I was led to a small room at the station where I could take rest and wait.

The Deogarh Raoji came in a *buggi* at about 5 p.m. We took a round of the famine-affected area. He dropped me at the guest house and left. By this time, the SHO Police of the area had come. I thought it was a part of his courtesy visit. But after Raoji had left, he gave me an alarming report. The advice given to me by Raoji of keeping myself off the village and confining myself to the station building was a part of Raoji's strategy. Chhotu Lal, the SHO reported that the tehsil building had been taken possession of by Raoji's men. It had been sealed by him and that his armed men were guarding the building and no government official was being allowed to enter.

### Unpredicted Predicament

The purpose of my visit was different, but since I had got the report of this rebellious act, I was duty bound to attend to it immediately. I gathered from the SHO, Deogarh, that the Deogarh *thana* had the staff of nine constables in all, but all of them were not available, three of them were on tour to the area in connection with some investigation, etc., and three were sick. The police station was virtually manned by a splinter staff of just three constables. A very disappointing situation! The nearest place where additional force could be available was the anti-dacoity picket at Dever, about 15 kilometres from Deogarh. I ordered the SHO to secretly send a messenger to Dever for additional force. But I knew that it would take time as the messenger would have to go on foot.

In a way, I was caught unawares and unarmed. We could not meet the rebellious jagirdar with force, but if the situation was allowed to continue, the authority of the government, at this sensitive stage, would be eroded. The only strategy open to me was to engage the jagirdar in some dialogue, at least for gaining time till the additional force from the anti-dacoity picket could be made available.

As a part of my plan, I enquired from Raoji about the situation through a local influential person. Raoji communicated back that he had not captured the tehsil office and that the armed persons around the sealed building were not his men. The communication was received through the same messenger; Raoji himself did not come. It was a significant point for me to note, for I could sense, that had Raoji been true in denying his involvement, he ought to have contacted me personally and explained his position. This point convinced me clearly that the report made by the SHO was correct.

## Constraining Conditions

Since I had to buy time till the additional force reached, I sent back the messenger with other queries giving the impression that I was not against Raoji or his lawfully accepted interests. There were exchanges of communication until midnight, and ultimately Raoji confessed that he had captured the tehsil office under his authority. He, however, conveyed that he would withdraw his men if I guaranteed that there would be no legal action against him. I as an administrator could hardly give such a guarantee, as this was neither within my powers nor was it advisable at that stage to do so. The only assurance that I could and did give him was that I would plead with the government to take a lenient view if he immediately withdrew his men and surrendered the building. He assured me to accede to my suggestion, and I pretended to be satisfied.

I could not sleep that night. The whole of my future and my family reputation—Mehtas had earned a great name in administration—appeared at stake. What would I do if in the morning I again found that Raoji had told a lie? The additional force had not reached by then, and I could not meet Raoji's men with the skeleton force of just three constables. If I personally went to check up the fact and physically inspected the building, this was likely to lead to vitiating the very cordial atmosphere that had been created after a long exchange of messages. The remaining hours of the night were used in planning and replanning the strategies for the next day with possible developments in mind.

The next morning, I sent a message to Raoji that I would like to make a courtesy visit to thank him before leaving. Promptly came his reply:

> Please don't come today. A number of jagirdars, drunk and furious, have collected here. Your presence may lead to untoward and undesirable incidents. I will myself come and meet you and see you off at the station.

I had no option except to wait for him at the guest house. Eventually, he came in his car at the train time and took me to the railway station, where we talked with each other while waiting for the train.

### Tension and Turbulence

The situation took a new turn when there appeared on the scene a mob of more than 500 men, armed with *lathis* and swords accusing, abusing and shouting slogans like '*Annadata ki jai*' (Long live the ruler-jagirdar), '*sadi-gali makka nahin khayenge*' (We won't eat rotten maize) and other anti-government slogans. They surrounded the station building while I was having talk with Raoji. At the same time, I got a confidential report from a CID personnel that the police station had also been surrounded by some armed men of Raoji and the SHO was virtually imprisoned. The situation was tense, and I became anxious. All alone, unarmed, no one to rescue me, I was a helpless person with a high burden of responsibility and a big challenge. What to do? Till then I had been keeping patience, but I felt as if I would lose it. And when Raoji asked me: 'What is the matter?' I lost my temper and exploded: 'Why ask me, you know better'. Raoji felt as if he had been exposed.

The mob wanted me to come out of the station room. I agreed to meet five to six representatives. The representatives demanded that the SHO should be suspended immediately since he had allegedly harassed the people. I could hardly have acceded to this demand. It was certainly not desirable administratively to act under pressure. However, I thought of making use of the situation and so offered to enquire into the matter personally after meeting the SHO. The mob relented. It was agreed upon that all would go to the police station and enquire.

Why did they make such a demand? The mystery was unravelled later. It was learnt that after the FIR (First Information Report) was registered with the police against Raoji for taking possession of the tehsil office and getting it sealed under his own signature, the SHO acted on this FIR and prepared the *panchnama*. For this, he pressurised a few reluctant persons to stand as witness to this fact. This was to serve as a documentary proof to establish the charge against Raoji, and therefore, Raoji's men demanded action against the SHO.

Followed by the crowd, as I was moving towards the police station, I was physically exposed to the unruly crowd. They were abusing and accusing me, calling names and shouting slogans. I was surrounded from all sides by the furious people, many of them intoxicated. A few of them cried: 'He is an agent of the government; he should not be spared'. As I was getting into the car, I saw a man trying to bring me under the range of his gun; others waving *lathis* and swords in the air. This was enough for a man to see his end approaching. I too felt panicky for a few seconds. But I had the strong faith in God and also in the ultimate sanity of the people. I had firm conviction in my mind that no harm would be done to me.

### Volatile Scene

Raoji probably had sensed the gravity of the situation. He smelled that the crowd might go out of control and some untoward incident might take place. That could lead to some fatal consequences. With a lightning move, he jumped on to the bonnet of the car and shouted, 'Stop'. He asked the people to allow me to go safely to the SHO. Raoji's intervention had an immediate effect. But the mob followed me to the police station. I felt a great relief when I reached the safe island—the police station—which was manned by the persons loyal to the government. It added to my relief when I found that the requisitioned anti-dacoit squad consisting of nine armed men had reached the police station. I entered the police station. Raoji asked: 'Should I come with you?' I said, 'You are welcome, I'll make the enquiry in your presence'. He accompanied me. Meanwhile, a rumour went through that Raoji had been arrested and detained by me. When I learnt this I had to ask Raoji to take leave, and I came up to the gate to see him off. The mob followed him. And then, I announced the result of my enquiry: 'The SHO was found not guilty'.

I was sitting on the roof with the SHO reviewing the situation. But within minutes, the mob returned with another demand that the paper seal signed by Raoji, which was pasted on the doors of the tehsil office and procured by the SHO with *panchnama* be returned. It further proved that the mob was instigated by Raoji who had started retreating in defence. As a part of the strategy, I pretended to accede to their request, and I asked for the paper seal from the SHO. I also gave certain indications that the SHO understood and handed over an equal-sized paper to me. I got it displayed to the mob down and got it torn off. I do not know how, probably because I accepted the demand immediately, the mob shouted that it was not the real paper seal and that they had been deceived. They started becoming violent. When my patience was exhausted, I decided that I should meet them with force. I immediately announced from the roof of the *thana* the promulgation of Cr. PC 144. I also sent a few copies of the handwritten notice for distribution among the people and getting it pasted. I noted that the people did not give any cognisance to it and rather tore off the copies. The mob was getting swollen minute after minute as there spread a rumour among them that I was not a competent authority to order police firing as the IGP (Inspector General of Police) was the only authority for giving such order.

## Commotion and Conclusion

The mob was getting violent. It was already getting dark and under the circumstances, some quick action had become imperative. There was no option left to me except to handle the situation with force, but internally I was not feeling safe. Rather I knew I was sitting on the top of a volcano; if the mob really got violent and threw a spark through the window of the room, we would all explode. The *thana* ammunition was stored in the very room down below us. Simultaneously, I took the next follow-up action. I ordered the SHO to get ready for firing position if the mob did not disperse within 15 minutes. But again, I hinted that SHO should not open fire till I gave specific orders.

This had a desired effect. There was a sort of commotion. People started discussing things among themselves. Their representatives requested me to give them 15 minutes time. I agreed but ordered them to be off the building to at least a distance of 100 yards. I saw a couple of persons rushing back, clearly to consult Raoji. As Raoji was completely exposed, and probably he thought it would be proper to surrender. Back came the message: 'The people should withdraw'. The mob started dispersing and within minutes it had moved away from the *thana*.

Next morning additional police force had reached us, and the situation was under control. I had to rush to Amet because such a situation had also developed there. However, before that I contacted the IGP on the phone. Probably the IGP had already received the alarming reports of the developments at Deogarh, and so he exclaimed joyfully, 'Are you still alive?' 'Yes, I am', I answered in a tone full of relief.

The IGP's words often remind me that I was saved by the providence. Why? May be because God wanted me to serve the people to the best of my ability.

# 3

# Mythological Rudder Collapsed

**Pradyumna Kumar**

'We were exempt from paying land revenue even in the times of Raja Hiranyakashyap. So it is not leviable on us even now. Come what may, we will not pay it to the government'. If such a bizarre claim is advanced even in the later half of the glorious twentieth century—to be specific in the year 1961—would it not sound shocking and surprising on the one hand and ludicrously exotic on the other hand. It was a lovely monsoon morning, and we consisting of a group of officers—Superintendent of Police, Additional Sessions Judge, Deputy SP, Treasury Officer and a few others—had just returned from a night out in a picnic in the vicinity of Jalore, a district headquarter, that a post-haste message was received that the entire Purohit community including womenfolk of village Santhu near Bagra had resorted to 'Dharna' in the village chowk. Our immediate reaction was to contact the Collector who a day earlier had left along with the Sub-Divisional Magistrate, Jalore, for another sub-divisional headquarters Bhinmal where a meeting was already scheduled. The telephone lines had been rendered unserviceable and the road blocked due to heavy rains. The only alternative was to seek help from the Railways to put us through. So the SP and I reached the railway station. The stationmaster, Jalore, contacted his counterpart at Bhinmal on their internal communication system, and it was through him that we could reach the local Sub-Divisional Magistrate and subsequently the Collector who came down to the railway station Bhinmal to talk to us. Thanks to the Railways that their alternate system worked and provided connectivity.

We apprised the Collector of the situation developing at village Santhu. The Collector instructed me to accompany the police force and local revenue officers as I was the only first-class magistrate available at the district headquarter in the absence of the SDM who was already with the Collector and unable to reach the spot immediately. When I conveyed this message to the SP, he immediately reacted by remarking that he would accompany only the District Magistrate. I was left with no option but to again contact the Collector, and it was on his specific instructions that the SP agreed to lead the police party along with me and some revenue officials.

We along with a truckload of force left for the spot without losing time. We found on reaching there that the entire Purohit community—men, women and children were quietly sitting in a common ground located in the centre of the village. The breast-fed kids were tucked in makeshift cradles with their ropes tied to the tree branches, their cattle driven to the pasture and houses left open and unguarded. The Sarpanch and other people approached us immediately with the plea that a solution to the problem was needed as it was growing increasingly difficult for them to guard the protesters' property and cattle in that situation. We even learnt that many of them had not eaten for a couple of days, and the kids also remained unfed for sometime. To top it all, a person had pierced a sword in his abdomen in protest and was lying in the same ground in a small tent guarded by a few community volunteers. It was a peculiar situation previously unseen and unheard of. The situation obtaining there did not pose an emergent challenge to the law and order, but it was certainly a determined and powerful collective expression of confrontation with the administration. Though peaceful in nature, yet it could not be ignored at all. It called for a deft handling without causing any provocation what-so-ever despite the fact that the demand was totally untenable.

In our party, there were two persons who knew the area, people and local culture—the Deputy SP, an officer risen from the ranks and Bishnoi by caste, and the Naib Tehsildar, a Rajput—both experienced and mature and having knowledge of the local social fabric. They located the important persons of the Purohit community and had a detailed dialogue with them. The Deputy SP emphasised to them that since the person who had thrust the sword in his abdomen was said to be in critical condition due to loss of blood, he should be persuaded to give his statement before any further aggravation in his physical condition took place, otherwise unnecessarily other persons of the community would be involved by law for abetment subsequently. His 12-year-old daughter sitting on guard with him was also emotionally tapped to agree to the legal requirement of having his statement recorded. The filial bond ultimately prevailed, and the person lying with a portion of dagger inside his body for over 24 hours relented to allow his statement to be recorded on the condition that no policemen would be around.

The Deputy SP told me about the situation. I asked him to let me talk to the people who had brought this message because I was the only person who was required to enter the ground and reach the tent where the wounded person or the 'hero' of the community had been lying surrounded by his followers. There was a risk of being made a 'hostage' in case something untoward happened. I persuasively told them that when they were with me I had no apprehension of any kind and that I could accompany them wherever they wanted. But they should also very well know that whenever a magistrate was on duty, he would always be accompanied by police. In this particular case, I would not take a number of them with me but at least one sub-inspector should accompany me so that I could perform my duty properly. They somehow agreed to this minimum requirement, and I along with a sub-inspector was escorted to the resting place of the 'hero' inside the tent enclosed on all sides by curtains.

What I saw inside was an unforgettable sight. A middle-aged, frail-looking person was lying on a cotton mattress spread on the ground with his minor daughter sitting by his side. A dagger about 18″ long entering about 2″ into his abdomen was clearly visible with blood clots and stains all around the wound. Nobody was allowed to extricate the dagger from his body, nor was any medical care called in lest it desanctified his vow taken in a temple of their community deity at a place called Kalindari in the adjoining Sirohi district after a religious ceremony called 'Tarkhad', which have been performed in the presence of a huge gathering of the Purohit community. The man was in his senses and could speak feebly. Nobody from his community and his nearest family wanted that he should be administered any medical aid or served appropriate liquid food for his sustenance even in that critical condition unless their demand was met in toto.

I sat with him on the ground along with the sub-inspector and expressed sympathy with him and slowly led him to narrate the entire sequence of events culminating in that extreme step. I also made him understand the implication of the statement to be made by him and also its benefits to his family and other members of the community in case something unwelcome happened to him as a consequence of the deep wound inflicted by himself in the middle of his fragile frame. His daughter also became emotional and persuaded him to have his statement recorded. In his statement, he mentioned how for the cause of his community he offered himself before a huge community gathering to undertake the 'Tarkhad' before the Devi at Kalindari temple, where he pierced his abdomen with the dagger after taking a vow that signified a fight to finish because the local authorities had not been conceding to their rightful claim sanctified by the mythology. I read over the statement to him and obtained his thumb impression, which also had traces of blood imprinted on the paper. We returned after wishing him well, and there was some lull for sometime, although eagerness appeared writ large on everybody's face because the demand was such that no one, not even the government, could accede to it for obvious reasons. However, behind the curtain, negotiations continued with the community leaders to make them come around to the only possible way out of the knotty situation that their demand would certainly be forwarded to the right quarters in the government for consideration and appropriate action taken after the matter was finally decided.

In the afternoon, I was sitting with the Naib Tehsildar and a few village folks outside a house in the proximity of the silent protesters observing their activities and the suffering they were undergoing by resorting to their 'Dharna' when I saw, to my dismay, that the police constabulary was being deployed by the SP to take position near the silent protesters to intimidate them. I immediately contacted the Deputy SP who was around and told him that the protesters had been peaceful all through and such an unnecessary show of strength was absolutely uncalled for. Anyway I would not become a tool if I was asked to pass some order later in case the situation turned unpleasant. The Deputy SP counselled the SP, and the force was withdrawn. However, everybody remained clueless as the ice was not melting.

It is perhaps for such intractable situations that the adage provides that where the human efforts fail it is the prayer that succeeds. The day was clear despite being rainy season, and the clouds were nowhere visible. But as the afternoon proceeded towards evening, the thick dark clouds laden with heavy showers started emptying themselves as if with a fury, and we saw there was an utter chaos all around. Soon the village cattle returning from the village pastures entered the place of 'Dharna' from all sides helter-skelter making the men and women run for their safety leaving the crying kids on the trees in their rope cradles. The small tent where the 'hero' was basking in the glory of his recent 'sacrifice' for the community had been flooded with rain water.

This sudden fury of nature totally unnerved the protesters and their leaders. The practical wisdom of the suggestion made earlier to them suddenly dawned upon them. The only question remained was the custody of the 'hero' who in the eyes of the law was an offender for the oblivious attempt to commit suicide. This problem was resolved when they were made to understand the legal complications if he died in their possession. They agreed for a medical aid sooner than later, and a doctor of the nearest government public health centre at Bagra, a small town, was immediately summoned by deputing a jeep for him in the pitch dark of the night with heavy clouds still looming in the sky. In the meanwhile, a message had already been received on the wireless from Bhinmal that the Collector and the SDM would also be reaching the Bagra railway station where the arrangement for their transport to reach village Santhu were accordingly made.

As soon as the doctor arrived, the first step was to remove the dagger from the abdomen of the 'hero' and provide all possible medical aid and also simultaneously complete all legal formalities by taking him in police custody. By the time these formalities were over, the Collector and the SDM had also arrived and were given complete brief of the day's happenings verbally. It was indeed an anticlimax to the irrationally whimsical drama. Both heaved a sigh of relief before we embarked on our return journey in the dark of the night along with the 'hero'—wounded not only physically but also morally with perhaps still deeper wound on his psyche—accompanied by his minor daughter and a couple of his close relations so that they could attend on him in the District Hospital where he was soon admitted on reaching Jalore late in the night. A criminal case was also registered against him for an attempt to commit suicide.

The actors of the script of this grotesque episode had perhaps never envisaged this comic relief, which not only led to the unexpected denouement but also made the entire community a synonym for ridicule. The mythological legacy of Raja Hiranyakashyap was unceremoniously buried deep forever.

Indeed, inscrutable are the ways of the God.

# 4

# On Looking Back

**V.B.L. Mathur**

It is my experience that with the passage of time, one has a tendency to focus on past events. Some periods of my service career are so vivid that it seems as if those happenings had taken place only yesterday. Therefore, while traversing the corridors of power, I have decided to go down memory lane to events that happened more than a quarter of century ago in terms of time but are very vivid before the mind's eye.

In 1961, I was the Collector of Jalore district. It was a very backward district with hardly any means of communication. The nearest metalled road went a few kilometres from the district headquarters of Jalore to the tehsil headquarters of Ahore. There was electric supply only in name in JaIore town, and there was no piped water supply in our homes. That year, September was a hot month, and I was sitting in my office in the collectorate waiting for the fan to start working, which it did for two hours every afternoon. My telephone rang and the operator informed me that the Special Secretary, Appointments, would like to speak to me from Jaipur. For a District Collector in 1961, and that too in a district like Jalore, a call from Jaipur and that too from the Appointments Secretary was enough to make one sit up in his chair. I picked up the telephone, and the first sentence I heard was such that I could hardly believe my ears. The Appointments Secretary informed me that I was to proceed to Simla on deputation with the Himachal Pradesh government. I was taken aback since I had not opted for central deputation and, for a moment, did not even realise that Himachal Pradesh was at that time a Union territory with its capital at Simla. I enquired as to what my assignment was and the answer came that he did not know. He asked me further if I were agreeable to the posting. Being in somewhat of a daze, I told him that I would ring him back after a little while. In fact, when the telephone call came, I had been busy dictating draft instructions for making arrangements in connection with the ensuing General Elections. I picked up the phone, an old battery-operated variety, and cranked it asking for my residence. I told my wife that I had been offered a posting in Simla. She thought that I was joking. On assuring her that this was not a joke, she said that I should not have even thought of discussing this with her but accepted immediately. I rang Jaipur and said that I would be only too happy to go to Simla. In fact, it was like a dream come true. I had just recovered from a very severe attack of smallpox, which had almost taken my life, and doctors had advised me to go to a cool place for complete recovery. With the kind of salary I got, it was impossible to think of a holiday in a hill station. However, I had spent many pleasant years in Simla as I had been educated there and had graduated from a local college in 1953. We packed immediately, and I handed over charge to the SDO, Jalore, lest the government should change its mind. We moved—bag and baggage—to Simla, and I joined there by the end of September 1961. On reaching there, I found that I had been posted as Registrar of Cooperative Societies and Secretary, Cooperative Department, as well as Director, Food and Civil Supplies, and Secretary, Food and Civil Supplies Department. The state was governed by a Lieutenant-Governor. There were only a few secretaries to government besides the Chief Secretary. After calling on the Chief Secretary and my colleague Secretaries to Government, I started getting acquainted with my job.

## Initial Expedition

Ever since I was posted as a Block Development Officer stationed in the village of Thanagazi in Alwar district, I had taken a lot of interest in the working of cooperative societies as I thought that these represented an alternative to the private and the public sector. I also thought that with an efficient cooperative system, the lot of the members of these societies could be significantly improved economically, and that economic betterment—which was the goal of the founding fathers of our Constitution—could be very well achieved through the cooperative system. I took a round of meetings over a month discussing with various officers different facets of the cooperatives' working in the then small Union territory of Himachal Pradesh. I found that they were generally performing work of routine nature. They visited cooperative societies, inspected their working and wrote audit-type critical notes on the societies' working. However, they did not seem to be doing anything concrete, which would improve the economic condition of the members of the cooperative societies. Among these officers, there was a middle-aged officer who struck me as very different from the others. He was bubbling with enthusiasm, and I thought his approach in suggesting solutions to problems was very practical. He was the Deputy Registrar in charge of marketing. I asked him as to what we could do to improve matters in concrete terms of economic gain to the people. He told me that if I were serious about this, I should take interest in the cooperative marketing of various agricultural and horticultural products since the cultivators were grossly exploited by middlemen or *arhtiyas* as he termed them.

I still remember the clear December morning and the azure sky as we got into our jeep parked below the Ridge and moved on to the upper heights of what was then called Mahasu district. Simla was a part of Punjab at that time, and we entered our territory only after leaving Simla town. The first night we halted at Theog where, from the Rest House at the top of a hill, we could clearly see the sun spreading gold on the snow-clad peak of Kinner Kailash in the distance and the murmur of the Lavi river flowing below us. As we sat that evening around a fire in the large drawing room of the Rest House, a number of seed potato growers came to meet us. Some of them looked very poor and were in tatters. I asked them why it was that though they produced seed potatoes, which fetched a high price in the plains, they did not seem to be prospering. They explained that though they produced large quantities of seed potatoes of the best possible variety, they never got a good price as their produce was purchased by middlemen at very low prices and then sold in the Simla market to buyers from other states at high prices. I told them that I planned to visit their areas starting next morning and would like some of them to accompany me on the trip, which was to cover the major seed potato growing areas of Mahasu district. For the next three days, I walked from early morning till sunset, climbing at times narrow goat tracks to the tops of mountains and visited not only villages but also far-flung hamlets. By evening, I was footsore and had blisters on my soles. However, we were young and full of enthusiasm and gradually a plan was getting formulated in my mind. On the fourth day, we reached a place called Khadrala, which was about 11,000 feet above sea level. I saw, dotted on the ground, large heaps of seed potatoes, which had been brought by villagers from far-flung areas. These were being purchased almost entirely by traders, and there were only a few cooperative societies and they seemed to be handling very small quantities only. The price being given to the growers was terribly low, and it was a price being dictated by the traders. The cooperatives were offering almost the same price, and therefore members were not coming to their depots. While talking to the cultivators, I found that they were completely in the grip of the traders, most of whom had a link with the village shopkeepers. The latter supplied essential consumer articles to the cultivators on credit throughout the year. To clear these loans, they had perforce to sell their seed potatoes and other produce at whatever price was offered 'by the shopkeepers'. These shopkeepers, in turn, sold or took the seed potatoes to Simla where they were sold at high prices to buyers from Maharashtra, Gujarat and other states where Himachal seed potato was highly prized since it was disease free, having been grown at very high altitudes. The most popular variety was 'Up-to-date Special', which was sold at a premium.

That evening, I held a meeting with a large number of potato growers in the lawns of the local rest house and outlined my plan of action. I told them that cooperatives should so organise themselves as to be able to purchase the potato produce of their members, which would then be handled at Simla by their Apex Federation, the Himachal Pradesh Cooperative Marketing and Supply Federation. They should also undertake to provide all essential consumer goods to their members throughout the year. The exploitation by the traders in selling essential consumer goods such as kerosene oil, sugar, tea, matches and edible oil was unimaginably high. Sky-high prices prevailed in villages during the winter and rainy months when communication with the supplying towns was disrupted and village shopkeepers exploited the growers in an almost cruel manner. The gathered cultivators told me that cooperatives had tried to sell their potatoes in Simla but had failed miserably as the *arhtiyas* controlled the market there, and the cooperatives had no say in dictating the market prices as the quantities they controlled were almost negligible. Till late that night, while relaxing before a fire of pine cones, I discussed with my Deputy Registrar, Marketing, how we would put our plan into operation. Next morning, I reached Simla and went straight to office and called a meeting of all the headquarter officers. We discussed, almost non-stop, for 6 hours. I also invited the administrator of the Himachal Pradesh Cooperative Marketing and Supply Federation, who was an officer nominated by the Registrar, Cooperative Societies. I found that the federation itself was in dire financial straits due to setbacks suffered in marketing agricultural produce in previous years. I also found out that if at all any cultivators got their seed potatoes to Simla to sell the stocks themselves, they were told that that day there was 'no rate', i.e., that no buyer in the market was prepared to buy the produce. The cultivators spent a few days in Simla and finally after having spent their money, which they could ill afford, would leave the potatoes behind with the *arhtiyas* requesting them that when the potatoes were sold, the money be sent to them less commission. As soon as they left Simla, the potatoes were sold at a very good price, but the farmers were sent only a paltry sum. There was a story going round in Simla that each *arhtiya* built one house every year on his yearly profit from the seed potato trade.

## The Strategy

I realised that it would be difficult to make any quick impact on such a highly controlled market and that we would have to change our battle plans. I found that seed potatoes of Himachal Pradesh were largely being purchased by Maharashtra, particularly by some of the cooperatives of Khed district. I picked up a young officer and sent him to Bombay and to Khed district to contact cooperatives and persuade them to buy directly from our federation. This young officer turned out to be a very skilful negotiator and, on return, told me that the cooperatives of the consuming district were quite willing to deal directly with our Apex Marketing Federation. Then, I did some research to find out as to how Simla *arhtiyas* kept the buyers under their control. I found that they were put up at traders' cost in a local hotel where they were wined and dined, taken for sightseeing not only around Himachal Pradesh but also to neighbouring hill stations of Punjab, such as Kulu, Manali and Dalhousie. However, we found that the buyers of Maharashtra were not satisfied with the quality of the seed potatoes sold to them. Deciding to do in Rome as the Romans do, we set up a committee under the chairmanship of the Deputy Commissioner, Mahasu, an IAS officer and old friend from Rajasthan cadre on deputation like me to Himachal Pradesh Government. The committee was given an entertainment budget of ₹ 10,000. They hired a hotel and put up the buyers there; their boarding and lodging was paid for by us and we also took them sightseeing though only in Himachal Pradesh. We built up a good rapport with them probably because we had better style in handling them.

Next I decided that we should offer the best possible stocks to our buyers. I wanted to demonstrate that the traders had been taking the buyers for a ride all the time and that our quality was far superior to anything that the *arhtiyas* could supply. I met the Chief Secretary, the Development Commissioner and the Director of Agriculture to whom I outlined my plan. They were enthusiastic and promised me full support. The Managing Director of Himachal Pradesh State Cooperative Bank agreed to provide the federation reasonable financial limits for purchasing seed potatoes from the cultivators. There were two clear areas where the best variety of seed potatoes was grown. These were Khadrala and Khara Pathar. I appointed two of our energetic officers as Loan Officers for these areas. I also got the Director of Agriculture to run a training camp for our cooperative staff to learn how to grade seed potatoes. These officials were deputed to the two areas and, after grading, they sealed each gunny bag with the federation's seal.

The graded seed potatoes were all kept at predetermined places, 80 per cent of the determined price was given in cash to the cooperative societies; 20 per cent was kept back since the federation provided gunny bags, *sutli,* transportation, etc. In the first season, we started our operations as there was heavy snowfall. Our officers had to carry large sums of cash to be disbursed to the members of societies. Many of them sat up all night to ensure that the money was safe. During the first season, the private traders did their utmost to sabotage our operations. We had arranged with the Transport Department of the government for trucks. But, trucks meant for us were generally diverted to the traders for obvious reasons by the Transport Department staff. I requested the Chief Secretary himself to see the operations. He agreed and toured the area for three days with us. The Transport Department got the message, and we had no trouble with them thereafter. I also persuaded the Railway Board to give 'C' class priority for rail movement of the cooperatives' seed potato. However, more trouble was in store for us. At the Simla railway station, the booking clerk created tremendous problems for us. Our wagons were parked away from the loading station on the plea that the track was under repair. At times, we found that the traders' wagons had been despatched at night while our wagons still had to be loaded. The electric light in the loading yard was switched off at 9.00 p.m. whenever our goods were being loaded. Otherwise, they were on the whole night. I had our loading contractor take care of the booking clerk, and we had no problem thereafter.

## The Pleasant Upshot

In the first year of business, the federation gave to the cultivators 200 per cent more than the price the cultivators used to secure from the traders. Even after deduction for the *bardana, sutli,* transportation charges, etc., they still had money coming to them, which we deposited in their names in separate accounts in the Cooperative Bank. Post cards were sent to each cultivator intimating him the amount deposited in his account and also details of the deductions. On top of the world with our successful first season, we organised the operation on more scientific lines thereafter. We stationed two officers in the states where we despatched seed potatoes. We had found that, at times, when the wagons reached their destination some bags of potatoes had rotted since they had been covered by snow or were wet when put inside the wagon. We showed our goodwill to the cooperative societies of Maharashtra by paying compensation for the spoiled goods. This was opposed by my officers who said that the buyers were present when the wagons were loaded, and therefore they should bear the loss. I explained to them that we must gain the goodwill of the buyers and we would benefit from this in the long run. This attitude did pay us handsomely. The federation's name for quality seed potato and honest dealing spread. Buyers from Gujarat and Karnataka also started coming to us. I started visiting the capitals of these states where the local Registrar of Cooperative Societies organised meetings with the representatives of the cooperative societies who were buying our potatoes. We discussed the arrangements we had made during the previous season and decided upon the line of action for the coming season. Later on, we found that it was important to secure information regarding the prices prevailing in these states during the seed potato season as the private traders of Simla had started under-cutting our rates. Every day, our officer, stationed in each buying state, would send us telegrams about the latest prevailing prices of various varieties of potato. However, to our shock, we found that the traders at times had the information before us. We discovered that they were intercepting our telegrams. We devised a code for various prices and qualities to get around this. By the third season, All India Radio was announcing the federation's prices in its daily morning and evening bulletins. The Himachal Federation's prices were generally 25–50 per cent higher per quintal than those offered by the traders and, by that time, more than 50 per cent of the market was controlled by the federation. I still remember, when I visited the villages in the seed potato producing areas in 1964, the villagers gave me a heart-warming reception. In one village, they composed a song in the local dialect about us and how we had beaten the *arhtiyas* and brought prosperity to the cultivators. It was certainly a time to remember, and we were delighted to see the prosperity, which was visible in villages where seed potato was being grown. Late at night, we sat with them around bonfires in village after village planning for the future.

Subsequently, we extended our marketing operations to cover seed potatoes being grown in Mandi district. But, we did not get the same success we had earned in Mahasu district. We then covered other agricultural produce such as ginger and chilgoza with considerable success. For the first time, the producers in the village were confident that they would get an economic price for their produce. We had also started ensuring that, before the potato market season opened, each cooperative in the village had sufficient stock of consumer goods for the entire winter.

It was, of course, a significant achievement that we were able to break the monopoly of the private trade in four years. At a national seminar, we organised on cooperative marketing, I read a paper on what we had achieved. My experience during the four years in Himachal Pradesh helped me a great deal in my later assignments in the Cooperative Movement, first in the central government, as Director of Consumer Cooperatives, and then as General Manager of the Delhi Super Bazar. The links forged between 1961 and 1965 with the simple cultivators of far-flung areas of Himachal Pradesh are still strong. Even after passage of decades, I get letters and invitation cards from some of them intimating me about weddings and births in the family. Once, when posted in Delhi, one of them came to meet me in Krishi Bhavan. My PA told me that the receptionist was worried and did not want to admit the villager wrapped in a blanket and smelling of sheep and goats. When he ultimately came into my room, Ladu Ram told me that he had come to see off his son who was going abroad. He said that he was doing well with his apple orchard and horticultural produce and could afford a good education for all his children.

My experience in Himachal Pradesh has strengthened my belief that those in power, if they are sincere and dedicated, can turn the tide in no uncertain manner and can even achieve the impossible.

# 5

# Threatened Confrontation Averted

**Sudhindra Gemawat**

It was a cold wintry morning. The sun had come up the horizon and was showering its warmth on the sand dunes of Barmer district. It was village Thob (of Pachpadra tehsil) where a large Kisan Rally was to take place. Congress Party had sent out invitation to all the cultivators of the district—particularly of Balotra Subdivision—where I was posted as Sub-Divisional Magistrate. This incident relates to the period between 1960 and 1963. The Agriculture Minister Shri Nathu Ram Mirdha was to address the gathering. Cultivators had come from far and wide to show their solidarity. The rift between the Jats and Rajputs was very much evident those days. Landlords and jagirdars were still very powerful and wielded great influence on village life. Rural folks would not dare to annoy the jagirdars. Most of the irrigated land was in the possession of Rajputs. Other communities had *barani* lands (unirrigated) in panchayats. In Panchayat Samities and Zila Parishads, Rajputs enjoyed majority.

Earlier, the meeting was proposed to be held in an open chowk of the village but as the hours went by, members of the Rajput community along with a big number of Thakurs and Jagirdars started moving towards Thob armed with swords, daggers and firearms. The number went on swelling. They all headed for the small fortress of the local Thakur, which stood atop a small hill.

A couple of weeks earlier, in a meeting of Congress workers, which took place at Samdari—a village in tehsil Siwana, the Minister, Shri Mirdha had spoken out against the Rajputs and jagirdars in particular. They were, therefore, very much annoyed at his outburst and wanted to show him their strength and power. We were duly informed of the visit of Hon'ble Minister and, therefore, the Deputy Superintendent of Police Shri B.K. Pareek and I had gone in advance to receive the minister and look for other arrangements. The police party had only eight constables with rifles.

When the organisers of the rally saw hordes of Rajput and prominent jagirdars coming to the village, the venue was changed from the open chowk to Bada (enclosure) of a Jat cultivator. This Bada had only one gate. The Minister arrived at about 10.30 a.m. as per the programme. He was given ceremonial guard of honour. When he was proceeding to the venue of the meeting, I apprised him of the situation and wanted to know if he would like the Rajputs to join the meeting or they should be kept away. Minister was shrewd enough and gave a diplomatic reply to use my discretion and judgement. I was in a dilemma and was quite perplexed for a moment.

If I stopped Rajputs from entering the Bada, there would be resistance and immediately a situation of conflict would arise. Besides all the Rajputs were well armed, whereas police force and personnel were only eight in number, which was quite inadequate to meet such a grave situation. As Deputy SP Shri Pareek was acting tough with the Rajput leaders, I requested him to keep calm and talk to them gently. They had already arrived at the venue and wanted to join the rally. When the talk between the Deputy SP and Rajput leaders was going on, I spotted Shri Himmat Singh Ji, Thakur of Jasol who was Pradhan, Panchayat Samiti, Pachpadra and a retired District Sessions Judge. I approached him and requested him to, somehow, avoid confrontation. He was a pleasant person and a gentleman. He said, 'It is a meeting of the agriculturists. We too are cultivators and have come to attend it. How can you stop us'. He showed me the pamphlet that was distributed by the organisers. I had no answer. With a prayer to God Almighty I told him, 'Yes, you can join the meeting' and allowed them to come where they had assembled earlier. They came in numbers and joined the meeting. By the grace of God, the meeting was completely peaceful. The minister softened his tone and this time, he seemed to be conciliatory and accommodative in his approach. Probably, he regretted his earlier remarks. The rally ended peacefully. We had a sigh of relief.

In retrospect, I shudder at the thought of casteist confrontation and its consequences. It was our good luck that we could return home happy and jubilant.

# 6

# Yes, I Recall

**Pradyumna Kumar**

With the passage of every fraction of a second, we keep on accumulating the past. Thus, the past keeps on getting heavier with fresh additions every moment, whereas the future only remains illusory holding promises to be realised later. So, it is only the past, which is ever present, offering us the wealth of acquired experiences shared with others or lived by ourselves. We only have to search into that vast treasure trove where the photostat copy of even our minutest experience is maintained. But this search has to be selective. Recalling the past for a particular purpose is to make an inward journey through those recesses of mind that may lead us to the specific source material. This exercise needs utmost care keeping in view the extent of time lag that invariably trends to blur the impressions. However, this should not deter us from making an honest attempt.

The earliest memory that comes to my mind relates to the first Panchayat elections held in early 1960 after the advent of Panchayati Raj on the 2 October 1959 in Rajasthan. During those days, I was undergoing my training in the Settlement Department at Alwar as the settlement operations were going on there only, although I was allotted district Tonk for the purposes of regular district training. So with a view to exposing me to the electoral process, the Collector of Tonk suggested to his Alwar counterpart for putting me through the drill. The job of the Returning Officer as I was designated involved right from receiving nominations, scrutiny thereof and conducting elections on the next day to counting of votes, declaration of results and administering oath to the elected ones. This required our stay of two days and two nights at the particular Panchayat headquarters.

I had some experience of conducting general elections of the Lok Sabha and Vidhan Sabha as a Presiding Officer in the second general election in Kota district in 1957 when both the elections were held together. So I did not feel scared of the new task ignoring the most important and crucial factor of local dynamics in the Panchayat elections, which was totally absent in the 1957 general election that I had earlier conducted.

After acquainting ourselves with the procedure of conducting the elections in a brief training programme at the district headquarters and collecting all polling material, our polling party reached the first destination as per schedule. Everything went well at the first polling station and then we left for the next destination having cosily spent two nights and two days there. The place arranged for our stay at the second polling station was not only unsafe for the polling material but also lacked adequate cover for the members of the polling party to probably insulate them from the severe winter. So we decided to shift to another public place belonging to a community on the suggestion of a seemingly respectable local person who incidentally happened to hail from that community. Next day at the time of filing nominations, it was revealed that he too was a candidate for the post of Sarpanch. Such situations in a small caste-ridden village society have the potential of causing serious troubles, particularly in a locally surcharged election atmosphere. It was as much an ignorance on our part as also perhaps our eagerness to hunt for a better place in a small village offering little options that we unconsciously preferred to let our official discretion remain dormant.

Next day, however, passed peaceful for our preparatory activities. On the succeeding day, the poll commenced on time with the voters turning up according to their convenience on the basis of two hours allocated for specific wards with 1-hour gap between each time slot. We the members of the polling party felt complacent with the process of poll heading peacefully, but soon it proved to be short-lived. A woman voter entered the polling booth having obtained her ballot papers—one for the ward member and the other for the Sarpanch—but she immediately came out shouting that the polling officers at the booth were themselves putting the seals on the ballot papers and the voters were not being allowed to cast their votes. A number of voters had already cast their votes before her, and no one had made such an allegation. Obviously, it was a sponsored plan with vicious intent. Soon there was commotion outside the polling station and the voters forming a queue left in protest indicating their resentment and boycott of the election process. For us this was something terribly unexpected. Our strong refutations of the malicious charge had little impact. In that situation, I was left with little clue. But then certainly I had advised my polling officers to keep their cool and that they should put on a bold face while remaining stead fast at their allotted seats. With a view to further maintaining their morale, I myself started moving within the demarcated area outside the polling station so that the village people watching us from outside might receive a proper message that there was nothing wrong with the election process.

When the first slot from 8.00 a.m. to 10.00 a.m. was almost over and I returned to my seat for sealing of ballot boxes, etc., of the relevant wards, a small mishap took place due to sheer inadvertence of a polling officer. In fact, when it was already 10.00 a.m. a voter belonging to the other group sneaked into the polling station for casting his vote. This was observed by a person who perhaps belonged to the opposite group, which had created the earlier ruckus. He raised a cry as to how a voter had been allowed when the time was over for the first set of wards. I had to again rush to the entrance of the polling station, which had the potential of aggravation in the earlier backdrop. I calmly but firmly told him that it was only the watch of the Returning Officer that regulated the election schedule and no one else's. Then I extended my wrist to him showing my watch that still there were 2 minutes left. This quick action silenced him. In fact, it was only the presence of mind that made me put my watch back by two minutes while moving from my seat to the entrance. Then I separately warned all the polling officers to be extremely careful in matters pertaining to elections.

Thereafter, we had a respite for an hour for our in-house work before the next slot, i.e., 11 a.m. to 1.00 p.m. allotted to the other set of wards. During this slot, the voters belonging to the other group slowly started trickling in for casting their votes but our apprehension was not yet over, particularly for the last stage when the result would be announced at 5.00 p.m. In the absence of means of communication during those days, we depended only on the visiting mobile parties to arrange and ensure for some police help in case of possible disturbance by the losing group.

Fortunately, a roving party of the Central Excise and Customs passing through that area had learnt about the situation developing at our polling station. The incharge of that party, although not directly concerned with the elections, had the courtesy to meet me on his way and offered if he could be of any help. I simply told him that we would try to tide over all minor difficulties during the poll but some force would be of immense help to us at the time of declaring results at 5.00 p.m. So, it would help us if he could inform some responsible police officer moving in the area about it. The man proved worthy of his salt and to our utmost relief the force was there at the requisite time.

In the meanwhile, the mere trickling of voters in the second slot had grown into long queues in the third and the last slot, i.e., 2.00 p.m. to 4.00 p.m. allotted to a tiny adjoining village demarcated as a separate ward of the same Panchayat. The voters of that village did not belong to the caste group of the Sarpanch candidate who had engineered the motivated disturbance in the morning through that lady voter. The result naturally went in favour of the other candidate as his voters turned out in great strength from the wards allotted to second and third slots. The winning candidate incidentally turned out to be the same person who had suggested the alternative place of stay preferred and occupied by us at that village.

It would, however, be worth recalling that the losing candidate, at last, expressed his satisfaction at the manner in which the elections were conducted and regretted that he was misled by some people. This compliment was perhaps a matter of greater satisfaction to the entire polling party than heaving a sigh of relief at our quiet exit from that village with all our bones intact.

But it would be my sheer vanity if I do not acknowledge the fact that this first thrilling experience during the training period could be gained by me only because of the deep personal interest taken by my training supervisor even from remote Tonk; otherwise I would have continued with the Amins and their chains in the village Mundia of Tehsil Malakhera undergoing my settlement regime prescribed by the Appointments Department as it was then called. This unique experience was my first objective lesson in handling the volatile situations, although I was only at the threshold of my administrative service career. Simultaneously, it also made me realise the valuable and unforgettable fact that indiscretion tempered with overconfidence has a tendency to lead to disaster. However, all is well that ends well.

# 7

# Once Upon a Time

**V.D. Sharma**

Nineteen sixty-seven was a crucial year in the political history of Rajasthan. The fourth general election in that year was an important event as during the period prior to that year, certain social, economic and political changes affecting the traditional life of influential sections of the community had been affected: *jagirs* and *zamindaris* had been abolished, and privy purses and privileges of the hereditary rulers were withdrawn. In the process of *jagirdari* abolition, the *jagirdars* had taken recourse to agitation and litigation, but the rulers of various integrating states had acted in a truly dignified and patriotic manner. In a very orderly way, they had surrendered their ruling powers to the new, democratic authority and were satisfied with some private properties left to them, privy purses guaranteed and the privileges permitted. Their attitude had rendered the transformation from a feudal and autocratic system to a democratic social order, peaceful and orderly.

There are some who believe that these events of transformation, when objectively judged by a future historian at a time when the prejudices of the present would die down, shall be hailed as a brilliant chapter of quiet self-sacrifice for a lofty cause. There are also some who believe that the actual process of abolition of the privy purses and privileges was not in full accord with the attitude and conduct of these scions of the princely order, and that the reform could have been better phased and undertaken in a less hasty and more sympathetic manner. Political events of this magnitude however come like floods. They do not always follow normal course. These abolitions, however, had their political repercussions and had at that time provoked angry waves of protest in the still waters of Rajasthan's political life.

## Ambiguity and Agitation

For the past several hundred years, the feudal elements of Rajasthan and the ruling princes of various states had been closely knit as a political entity and the two were complementary to each other and interdependent. Even these rulers whose states were formed at different periods of history, during the Mughal and the British rule, became the feudals of the Delhi *Darbar* and had created within their respective territories further feudatories in the form of *jagirdars,* big and small. The interests of all these were adversely affected by the dawn of democracy and by the various measures of reforms. This happened before 1967. Their efforts to undo these reforms through litigation in courts, etc., have not achieved any success, they thought of fighting out the powers responsible for the reforms through political action. These forces therefore combined just prior to the year 1967 to give the ruling party tough fight during the general election. An all-India party known as Swatantra Party was organised under the stewardship of Chakravarti Rajagopalachari and in Rajasthan, a number of opposition parties collected under the banner of this new party. In the elections, the new combination had a fair measure of success in Jaipur district where I was the Collector as well as the District Electoral Officer at the time.

The election results showed that the margin between the ruling party and the combined opposition was very narrow indeed, and this resulted in lot of 'horse trading' or defections. There was the usual parading of supporters and rival claims to majority till at last the Governor of Rajasthan gave his verdict in favour of the then ruling party at the centre, i.e., the Congress Party and the combined opposition reacted to this decision through a widespread agitation.

## Reluctance to Be Released

In the course of the agitation, a large number of workers of the opposition parties including leaders such as Bhairon Singh

Shekhawat, Master Adityendra, Satish Chandra Agarwal, Hari Krishna Vyas, Kumbharam Arya and Ramkaran Joshi were arrested. A considerable number of workers were arrested not only for breach of prohibitory orders but also for acts of vandalism, stone pelting and the like. The above leaders were however arrested for breach of prohibitory orders. The state government later took a decision that all cases of breach of prohibitory orders be withdrawn and people arrested for only such breach be set free. It was also decided that cases against those arrested on charges of violence be proceeded with. As a result of this general decision, cases against all the opposition leaders were withdrawn, and they were consequently to be released from jail.

When the Superintendent of the Jaipur Central Jail proceeded to release the opposition leaders, they firmly told him that they would not step out of the prison until all persons arrested during the agitation, including those arrested on charges of violence, were released. The then District Magistrate of Jaipur used to be the supervisory officer of this prison and the position taken by these leaders was reported to me by the Superintendent. I visited the jail and discussed the matter with all those leaders, but they continued to be adamant in their stand. The matter was reconsidered by the state government in the light of this situation, and the government came to the conclusion that it could neither accept the stand taken by the leaders that they would not step out of the prison unless other people were simultaneously released nor could it accept the right of these persons to stay in the prison at their will even when there were no charges against them under which they could be held in custody. Certainly, there were chances that these people would later claim that the government continued to keep them in custody even though no charges of any kind were outstanding against them. The government therefore decided that the policy of withdrawal of cases could not be further extended.

I wrote to the Superintendent of the Central Jail to inform the leaders in jail of the decision of the government to release them forthwith, but he later told me that these persons had firmly refused to budge from the position they had taken.

## The Political Imperatives

Though the Governor had decided to install the government of Mohan Lal Sukhadia in a provisional way, the latter had been asked to demonstrate his majority in the Vidhan Sabha within a prescribed period, and this period was to expire shortly. The government was therefore anxious to release these leaders as early as possible so as to avoid any complication, which might arise from their absence from the House.

All persuasions to make these leaders agree to leave the prison had failed and one afternoon, the Chief Minister, in the presence of the Chief Secretary, personally conveyed to me his anxiety in the matter. I assured him that I would do my utmost to get these people out of the prison that very day.

## Designing the Action Plan

I planned the operation carefully and took the then Superintendent of Jaipur prison, Amar Singh Ranawat—who later retired as IG of prisons—into confidence. I told him that I would be visiting the jail that evening and the same should be treated as my formal visit. I told him that my arrival should be announced by a group bugle-sound technically known as 'rivoli' and that seating arrangements should be made in a room having a raised platform where I would sit, with my audience occupying the ground-level chairs. Wardens would be made to stand guard on the entrance of the room and a serene atmosphere like that of a court room would be created. The room chosen was to have a back door and another attached room. A group of about 20 wardens selected for their fitness, stout physique and big moustache should wait in that back room to be readily available and to suddenly emerge in the main room when a signal for the same is given.

These arrangements having been properly made, I along with my friend L.C. Gupta—who was then my Additional DM and who himself later became DM, Jaipur—reached the jail premises. Because of the disturbances, there was curfew in the town, and therefore I took a few other magistrates on duty with vehicles and a few spare curfew pass cards with me.

## Punctilious Enactment

The plan was cautiously carried through. I reached the sitting room along with L.C. Gupta and asked the Jail Superintendent to conduct all these resistant leaders to the room. They were all important public men and my relations with them were of cordiality and respect. They came and greeted me with the usual warmth but since I had to carry out a particular project, my response to their greetings was absolutely formal and placid. They naturally asked me about the decision of the government on their condition for the acceptance of the release, namely, the simultaneous release of all prisoners, including those who were convicted for offences involving violence. I informed them in a formal tone that the government decision in the matter will be just announced to them and it was for that very purpose that they had been called.

After they were all seated, I announced to them in a most business-like and authoritarian tone that the government had considered their viewpoint and had taken the decision that cases on those who had been confined on account of conduct involving 'violence' shall stand and will not be withdrawn and that persons against whom cases have been withdrawn have no right to stay on in the prison. They should therefore be released forthwith.

The opposition leaders tried to argue with me the various implications of the problem and did not seem to agree with me. Further, they wanted their stand to be further communicated to the government. I however told them firmly that the government decision was made after fullest consideration of all aspects of the problem and that it has to be complied with and no further arguments against such compliance could be heard. If they felt that anything wrong had been or was being done, they could themselves approach the government after their release. With these words, I stopped all further arguments and told them to decide within 5 minutes if they would willingly walk out of the prison or not.

One of the audience, probably Bhairon Singh Shekhawat, asked me as to what will be done if they stuck to their resolve not to leave the prison. I replied that I sincerely hoped they would themselves decide to walk out of the prison but in case they opted not to do so, I need not announce the next step, which they would themselves see when taken. They had some consultation among themselves and firmly told me that under the circumstances, they had decided not to leave the prison.

The next phase followed as per my plans. I called upon the Superintendent of the Jail to proceed with the next step. Instantaneously, the door of the room at the back flung open and the opposition leaders in the room found themselves surrounded by a host of tall and stout wardens. I told the audience that they must have themselves comprehended the next phase, which they may perhaps like to avoid. I felt happy that these gentlemen readily grasped the implications of the situation and agreed to leave.

### Felicitous Finale

At this crucial point, I thought of doing something to break the tension generated by this situation and therefore asked the Superintendent of the prison to order for tea and snacks so that the parting moments are without much tension. In fact, even this arrangement had been kept ready. I got down from the pedestal where I had seated myself and came and sat among these friends. We fully enjoyed our tea and exchanged pleasantries with each other.

Having finished this happy meeting at the tea table, the opposition leaders were sent home in official vehicles after affectionate greetings. As stated above, they were important persons in public life with some of whom I had long-standing relations. Several of them later rose to positions of state government ministers and other dignitaries, and one of them became the Chief Minister of the state. I feel so happy to relate that this event never cast any shadow on the relations of warmth and mutual regard we had during the rest of my service and even after my retirement. These political leaders continued to be kind to me perhaps because of their appreciation that the occurrence was one occasioned by the peculiar exigencies of the situation and that there was no lack of goodwill on either side.

# 8

# The Deluge Dilemma

**I.C. Srivastava**

Memory unveils another law and order eventful nightly vigil. It relates to the likely cataclysmic catastrophe to Bharatpur town on the 14–15 August 1969 arising from swirling floodwaters filling Ajan bund to the brim. For a few days, Ajan bund had been receiving inundated rain from Bayana tehsil and beyond in the catchment area of the river.

In the wee hours close to 2 a.m. on 15 August 1969, Shri Vinay Vyas the then Collector, Bharatpur, driving himself in a jeep arrived at my residence while I was posted as SDO Bharatpur. Shri Vyas woke me up to tell the following: (a) he was proceeding to Dholpur immediately to persuade a man on fast-unto-death hunger strike to give up the same and resume taking food so as to avert his death; (b) I should leave for Ajan bund located at one end of the world famous Ghana Bird Sanctuary accompanied by Shri P.N. Khanna, IPS under trainee who had already been instructed by the then District SP Shri Narayan Singh to take a truck load of police force; (c) on account of floodwaters inundating various villages, people had collected and parked themselves on the service road of Ajan bund alongwith their belongings and cattle sensing their insecurity in the flooded villages; and (d) as the fast moving flood waters of Gambhiri had been filling Ajan bund, it was likely to endanger Bharatpur town located 10 km away from the bund. To deal with and tackle the crisis situation, if necessary, the people sitting on bund could be forcibly removed before resorting to demolishing a portion of the Ajan bund.

As he had little time for any further discussion, I could only plead with him to take one or two armed constables with him as the Dang hilly and forest road he was going to drive through was dacoit infested and hazardous. He accepted my advice against his typical habit of driving himself alone any time of day or night, somehow though allowing the driver to jump into the back of the jeep as he made the whirring starting sound.

Immediately after the Collector had left Shri P.N. Khanna, ASP (he was later posted as District SP in 1976–1978, during my tenure as Collector, Bharatpur) arrived with the police force and we started for Ajan bund without losing any time. In the dark, rainy night, we had only jeep headlights to guide our way. At the eastern end of Ajan bund, Shri Mahesh Narayan Bhardwaj, the then Executive Engineer, Irrigation, was sitting on a cot dressed up in knee-level shorts. He asked us to take stock of the situation prevailing on the bund and gave no further advice on how to face or tackle the situation. After driving about half a kilometre on the slippery, muddy road of the bund, we could see the dark shadowy figures of villagers and cattle huddled up in awe and despair. We left the jeep and as we reached the middle of the 3 km long bund, an unforgettable and awe inspiring scenario emerged before us; the heart seemed to sink in the fury of floods which rushed and gushed down like large sheets in the form of cataracts through 28 sluices of the iron gates making thunderous and high gurgling sounds on striking 20–30 feet ground below. The whole scenario seemed to be, somehow, reminiscent of the 'deluge' of the Bible and Pralaya of Hindu mythology. We could imagine the likelihood of people including women and children losing their lives in the unkind nature's fury by being swept away in the over topping swirling waters. As this possibility loomed large in our minds, it struck us as well that crashing of any dam structure portion on Bharatpur side would allow flood waters to rush towards Bharatpur town and then we would meet the same fate as the villagers.

Shri P.N. Khanna gave me full support and apparently to keep up morale, he began to smoke a cigarette. Watching his cool demeanour and equanimity, it struck me that we would be well advised to enlist the support of Shri M.N. Bhardwaj before taking any decision. As a law and order situation has to be first tackled and overcome on the spot after which papers are prepared, we had naturally forgotten to bring pen and paper with us. However, with the help of a pencil I sent a small note on the inside of the cigarette box to Shri Bhardwaj whether it was essential to break the bund keeping in view the rising level of water on the lower side of the bund and asked for his views so that we could consult him further. A seasoned and experienced officer as he was, Shri Bhardwaj chose to remain mum and we kept waiting for his message for half an hour.

It was a matter of chance or godsend opportunity that a junior engineer of Irrigation Department suddenly appeared before us and advised that perhaps it would not be necessary to resort to break any bund wall as in his assessment the water level had become stable by that time. He reassured us that he would make an estimation of the water levels in different parts of the bund and come back to us before early morning and then he would be able to spell out his views clearly. He kept his promise and came back at 4.30 a.m. By then, early twilight had somewhat removed darkness. He remarked, 'Sir, please accept my advice, I cannot give any guarantee but I can only say that it is not necessary to go for breaking the dam because flood water is fully stable now and rains have also stopped in the upper reaches of the river'.

To us, then, that Junior Engineer appeared to be an angel sent by God for there was no other information or data readily available nor was there any other way out of the situation. The dumb-founded attitude of Executive Engineer had, in fact, become a hindrance in our view but his subordinate official gave us a memorable counsel that facilitated our taking correct decision in the situation. For us, it was an unforgettable night which confronted us with an unprecedented situation. We expressed our deep gratitude to God Almighty for retrieving us from that precarious situation, which endangered the safety and security of lives and property of hundreds of people besides the threat posed to Bharatpur town. On our way back, we conveyed to Shri Bhardwaj our admiration of Junior Engineer for his sagacity and correct advice.

As we had to get ready early for the 15th August Independence Day Parade, we returned home quickly. As Collector had proceeded to save the life of a person on hunger strike, District SP took the salute at the march past parade.

That deadly night ushering in 'deluge' like dilemma for us remains sharply etched in my memory as if the event had happened yesterday. I am thrilled and filled with awe in thinking as to how we could face and live up to the need of the hour in that crisis full of dilemma. To me, it was a unique and rich administrative experience that inspired me to remain fearless and cool to take balanced view before taking decisions.

# 9

# An Unenviable Election Night

I.C. Srivastava

March 16, 1969 was an unforgettable and eventful day of my life. As Sub-Divisional Officer, Bharatpur, I had to conduct Krishi Upaj Mandi Elections of Nadbai tehsil and it turned out to be a memorable experience. Paharsar, a large village of Nadbai Tehsil lies at a distance of 25 km from Bharatpur on National Highway No. 11, towards Jaipur. Before 1947, it was a predominantly Muslim populated village but was later occupied by refugees from Pakistan after the migration of Muslims whose dilapidated and tell-tale *Havelis* are a grim reminder of the gruesome events of the partition of the country. But, the widespread political awakening was reflected in the keen contests of candidates in the first ever Krishi Upaj Mandi elections.

Time appeared to be standstill to watch the politically awakened masses participating with clamorous excitement in this very local election process amidst the din and rush of vehicles and loudspeakers, which clearly reminded us of the days of parliamentary and State Assembly Elections; in this election expenditure flowed into several lakhs almost at par with general elections, for electing seven candidates in all. Tractors laden with flags and supporters of candidates tore and roared their way across villages. Rumours floated about detention of voters at few villages followed by unconfirmed messages. But the climax occurred towards the evening for me and my colleagues and posed a great challenge, which was faced and overcome with intelligence, courage, some luck and, of course, grace of God.

In Paharsar village, the polling station was located in a small room of the primary school, which had only one door for entry and exit of nearly 1,500 electors. Election procedure was more complicated than that of general elections. Each voter made to sign and cast seven votes by stamping seven times on a large ballot paper containing names and symbols of 45 candidates was expected to take at least a minute to complete this process up to folding and dropping that ballot paper in the box. At 4 p.m., I received the message that polling had been stopped at Paharsar polling station as the gathered crowd had become unmanageable. According to rules, polling had to be closed at 5 p.m. Arriving there in a jeep with four police constables, I found that the polling party was sitting quietly and huddled up after calling off the polling. Outside the boundary wall, swelling crowd of over 1,000 persons was clamouring and shouting to be allowed to vote.

To begin with, my accompanying constables took their positions replacing those deployed but were already too tired to continue. As a Sub-Divisional Officer it was my bounden duty to get the whole election process completed and I focused on the same with some impromptu devices and immediate action. Some employees suggested calling off the poll entirely as votes could not be cast in that critical law and order situation. Then, I remembered Nehru's words, 'success often comes to those who dare and act' and plunged myself to the task at hand. As per the election procedure, everyone present in the polling premises and remaining to cast vote was entitled to do so. But lack of staff to distribute slips and also to distinguish voters in the crowd prompted me to shout at the top of my voice, 'everyone will have the right to vote if separate queues are formed villagewise and voters sat there to wait for their turn'. The blind and the handicapped were allowed to form a separate queue and asked to vote on priority basis. As there was only one gas petromax lantern, it became difficult to control the crowd in the growing and surrounding darkness. The police constables left their posts and positions and the crowd turned uncontrollable. It was already 6 p.m. and nearly 700 voters were waiting for their turn.

Suddenly, I stood on top of a table with the gas lantern in hand much like a character in the novel *A Tale of Two Cities* by Charles Dickens and challenged the crowd in a bold high-pitched voice, 'A mother's pan takes only one loaf (Roti) at a time to bake and roll out and each child has to wait for his turn to receive the same. Every thing including voting takes time. If everyone remains quiet and cooperates, it will take less time'. Voters' names were announced by shouting and it was 11 o'clock at night that we decided to give up that device as possibility of some non-voters being allowed in could not be ruled out in that process.

The crowd was swelling by the minute and it was becoming well-nigh impossible to control them. All employees on duty were continuously working without taking food and water. Policemen too were alert and ready to discharge their duties again. But it flashed in my mind that the device and method adopted would not complete the process even by 10 o'clock next day. Hence, I decided to appeal to people to vacate the premises and stand outside the boundary wall. Man is accustomed to follow a social ordering and system. Everyone complied with my fervent appeal and I deployed the four constables to stand along the wall and I myself sat on a chair at the small gate around midnight under the dark and cold sky. Someone thoughtfully placed a blanket on my shoulders. From the swirling crowd, I would pull one voter inside at a time and everyone got his turn by 4 a.m. when I could declare the polling closed. All workers weariness reflecting on their faces felt highly satisfied having fulfilled their promise to voters.

Democracy embodied and writ large on faces of voters reflected its own glory and power in those hours of night and left an indelible impression on my mind. I still wonder and try to figure out the strange innate power that gave me enough strength and courage to carry out the onerous and pious task of holding the polls for farmers' own mandate to govern themselves through their Krishi Upaj Mandi Samiti. How could my colleagues and workers devote themselves to their election duties hungry and thirsty as they were for long hours? Was it only on account of awe and aura of sovereign power of the state? It is my conviction that all this was accomplished with the deeply embedded inspiration of the spirit of democracy for government and governance represent and embody that disembodied spirit of social order. It is—it is certainly a memorable experience for me.

Inspired and enthused as we were alongwith the staff, the event gave us enough strength to work continuously for sixteen hours and only after declaration of election results, we could derive real pleasure and satisfaction on having achieved our tasks. Before announcing the election results, I appealed on mike to the gathered crowds outside the hall, 'all the people should go home peacefully after declaration of the results'. Use of force, including firing as per requirement of the situation, also formed part of my speech and appeal. At that hour, the people of Bharatpur would follow only the loud and clear warning. Hence, the situation turned out to be on the expected lines and the people dispersed peacefully.

# 10

# Fighting the Flames and Visit to Parbat Ali

**I.C. Srivastava**

December 8, 1971: Time 11.35 p.m. Indo-Pak War Theatre: Barmer Railway Station, Rajasthan. It may be recalled that after the outbreak of Indo-Pak War on the December 3, 1971, Barmer district (area over 28,000 sq. km, larger than many European Countries and then encompassing the world's largest election constituency in the largest democratic country, India) witnessed a series of bombing operations by Pakistani war planes flying out from Badin airfield in the Western Sector. On the very first day, at night, Pak planes had destroyed an HF aircraft at nearby Uttarlai airfield killing an airman. After randomly and intermittently bombing border tehsil town Chohtan and the bed of a rural water tank near Pachpadra Tehsil headquarters shimmering and glimmering white in the night between the 3 December and 7 December, a major air assault was mounted by Pak war planes at Barmer railway station on the night of 8th December 1971. As ex-officio Civil Defence Controller in addition to my duties as District Magistrate, Barmer, during the period December 1970–September 1972, it was a part of my essential duties to inspect and find out, first hand, the impact and the damage caused by enemy air sorties and bomb shelling.

Shri Shantanu Kumar, the then District SP Barmer (who eventually rose to be Director General, Police Rajasthan) picked me up to drive us to railway station in his jeep. There we witnessed a most horrifying and terrible spectacle—railway godowns burning and flames rising from the tracks and goods wagons stationed at the railway station. Although no casualties could be noticed in that horrific hour, we could not help feeling and anticipating the impact of the bombing. We were also overwhelmed by the spirited action of the local citizens who had not only come forward in large numbers but also organised themselves on the spur of the moment in groups armed with hammers and buckets full of water—hammer to unhook and separate the burning wagons so as to prevent further damage and water to put out the leaping flames. It was highly motivating and inspiring to see the citizens acting in concert and unity in that emergency, which was mainly to prevent the leaping flames from spreading towards two cinema halls and nearby town areas.

Someone from the crowd informed us that water not being available in plenty sand from sand dunes located near the town would be more effective in fighting the napalm bomb flames. An expert civil defence officer had already advised us on this issue and arrangements had been made to transport sand-filled trucks to the railway station. One such truck was already on its way. For us it was then, 'lo and behold face to face near brush with death' when this truck fully loaded with sand was, in all likelihood, going to ram into our jeep in the pitch darkness enforced by curfew but was saved by the last moment quick and intuitive split second swerve of the steering wheel by Shri Shantanu Kumar, which diverted the movement of jeep towards a telecom pole hitting the side of the jeep. It was a providential and hair breadth escape for us after nearly landing, so to say, into the jaws of death. We were then back to operate from our underground 'katcha' bunkers (10′ × 10′ × 10′) at home.

This unforgettable event embedded in my memory will always remind us of the heroic endeavours of citizens of Barmer town, whom I addressed next morning, on the simultaneous broadcasting network already laid all over the town, to congratulate them for the previous night's labour of patriotic love and also to raise their morale during that ongoing war situation. It was gratifying to be informed later in the day that my appeal on the mike and vivid narration of the valiant saga of their brethren and fellow citizens by me did raise the morale and spirit of the people especially from business community, who had started fleeing the town in buses. Government officers and their families living in the residential colony who were braving the likely bomb-shelling day in and day out also set an excellent example for other citizens to follow. When the exodus of business community stopped, people came to me in delegation to seek night protection and air cover by our own war planes. We had already spoken to officers in air command headquarters at Jodhpur and were assured of the air protection to be provided by MIG-19 planes. They landed the same afternoon by announcing their arrival with a bang made by their breaking sound barrier. Needless to add, people were fully reassured of the air protection and our air force's ability to keep the enemy planes at bay after the 9th December. However, in day time on the 10th December 1971, a 'dog-fight' between IAF 'Gnats' and Pak air force planes took place over Uttarlai air field at about 9.30 a.m. in the morning, which proved to be another memorable and unforgettable event in the war history of Barmer because our smallish looking Gnats not only gave a good fight but also finally chased away enemy planes.

## Ceasefire and Visit to Parbat Ali, Army Occupied Territory

After the ceasefire was declared on 16 December 1971 at the end of 1971 Indo-Pak War, the then Chief Minister, Rajasthan, Shri Barkatullah Khan announced that he would hoist the Indian tricolour flag at Chachro Tehsil headquarters, which he did perform ceremoniously shortly. Indian army had captured and occupied nearly 8,000 sq. km of Pak areas falling in Chachro and Nagarparkar tehsils of Tharparker district. In fact, Major General R.D.R. Anand who had himself advanced in the occupied area in his 'Caravan' vehicle alongwith his troops had informed me about all important features of the area at 2 a.m. on 19 December 1971 through the newly laid telecom lines on the sand dunes from somewhere near Naya Chhor in Mirpur Khas district from where the green belt of Pakistan was clearly visible. General Anand had invited me to see for myself the vast, sprawling areas captured by Indian army, which were awaiting some semblance of Civil Administration for the welfare of the Meghwals and Rajputs who were still holding forth in their villages despite having been caught in the crossfire of the fighting armies of two nations. Food ration and other civil supplies had to be rushed there. Hence, General Anand invited me to see the area and organise the despatch of essential supplies of foodgrains and medical aid.

In the last week of December 1971, I could not resist seizing once-a-lifetime opportunity of visiting some occupied area of Pakistan. A route chart alongwith a travel plan in a 'secret' marked cover was brought to me personally by an army officer. A station wagon made of jeep with a four wheel drive was requisitioned for my travel alongwith my PA Shri Mangi Lal, PRO Shri Bhoor Chand Jain and a gunman for protection. We travelled by road up to Munabao and left the station wagon behind to negotiate the newly laid steel duckboard tracks along the sandy terrain marked by rural Kachha Rasta and went aboard a standing two compartment railway train, which made its way to Khokhrapar, Vasarwa, Jaluchara and Parcheji Beri Pak railway stations. At a small railway station named Anand, we temporarily alighted from the train and resumed our journey in the station wagon. We patiently negotiated our way up the sand dunes, which kept steadily rising with the frequent use of 4 × 4 wheel drive. We slowly realised that the highly secured fenced duckboard track was made after our army had cleared off the mines laid by Pak army in order to prevent the fighting advance of our troops. It was brought to my notice that Brigadier Katara had lost his both legs somewhere there while advancing on mine filled sandy tracks during the war.

War-inspired awe and fear seemed to fill our hearts and minds while we put up appearances of fearless faces and calm demeanour. Up and up the sand dunes, as we made our way, dunes turned into high hillocks that too transformed into low hills ranging from 500 ft to 1,500 ft and more. The high point or peak of Parbat Ali was reached at 1 p.m. from where the township of Naya Chhor and adjacent villages were clearly visible in mist cleared day light. Life as usual in that vast area was to be seen to be believed. A flour mill with smoke billowing from hidden diesel engine and a mosque with men offering prayers were two objects that completed the picture of vastly spread rural urban mixed scenario. Green fields on the edge of sand dunes stretching into the brown sandy valley could be made out with a naked eye too and were visible clearly in the army binoculars provided to us.

What a historic and momentous spectacle it was to visit and see Parbat Ali and have ourselves photographed on the summit, immediately after the historic conquest by Indian army, of an area that was to be returned after July 1972 Simla agreement signed by India and Pakistan! Highly satisfying as it was, the visit was rounded off by a more satisfying quick lunch so thoughtfully laid by army officers in the temporarily set up officers' mess. Happily and fortunately for us we came back safe and in one piece to Munabao our border village and to Barmer, the district headquarters at night the same day. Bon homie generated between army, air force and civil officers during the war lingered in memory and lasted for a long time until we lost touch in the hum drum and crowded world of our own, over the years.

# 11

# An Unexpected Encounter

**I.C. Srivastava**

After going through the fierce trials and travails of Indo-Pak War (December 1971), my role as Collector and District Magistrate, Barmer, extended to providing immediate relief to refugees from Pakistan areas, who had literally walked into India from Indian army occupied territories which included the whole of Chhachro tehsil and parts of Nagarparkar and Mithi tehsils of Tharparker district of Pakistan. The relief work was organised on war footing by: (a) commissioning PHED tubewell points for locating camps for refugees, (b) drawing over ₹ 6 lakh in instalments under Treasury Manual (Rule 27) empowering Collector for such emergent contingences, (c) sanctioning rations under an earlier circular of GoI laying down scale of dal, oil, sugar and wheat, etc., and (d) promoting Patwaris as Inspector Last Records (ILR) and ILRs as Naib Tehsildars—such an initiative was never questioned for I had informed both Government of Rajasthan and GoI on the action taken and no explanation was ever asked for all steps taken during and in the aftermath of war.

However, administrative system takes its own grind and milling as the routine work catches up with the officer. Higher officers too expected yearly inspections to be completed before the end of 31 March 1972. Hence, the quick round of inspections and night halts followed through. One evening in March 1972, on arriving at Bakhasar Police Station, the southern tip of Barmer district (which looks like a cape on the district map which itself seems to be a replica of India map), I witnessed a most remarkable spectacle which is still etched in my memory and is apparently worth sketching in words. A knight-in-armour's horse highly gilded and glimmering and glowing in the last rays of sun and basking in its glorious and glamorous appearance in upright posture formed a rare spectacle, which is embedded still in my memory. As I alighted from the car, I found no one near the solitary horse. But soon enough, lo and behold its master, Thakur Balwant Singh hastily came out from the arched courtyard of the police station and greeted me with Marwar greeting 'Khamma Ghani' and a Rajput's chivalrous, slight bow paying his obeisance and respect to the institution of the District Head that I represented. Balwant Singh was an ex-dacoit who was a terror across desert areas of Indian subcontinent before surrendering to Rajasthan Government after 1965 Indo-Pak War. He also helped Indian army in 1965 war. I admired his horse and asked him a few questions about the décor, upkeep and the beautiful saddle and other accessories which together gave the horse its traditional fairy tale appearance.

More surprise awaited me as I turned around to go inside the police station. SHO though well built looked rather sheepish as he paid his respects and followed Balwant Singh and me. It was Balwant Singh and he alone seemed to command the affairs of the police station for he escorted me to inspect each room explaining everything in great detail such as goods and materials stored in Malkhana, the weapons and arms in the armoury besides Havalat and the room meant for the Special Police Officers, i.e., civilians recruited by the District SP to render assistance in keeping vigil on the borders besides collecting intelligence on cross-border activities. Balwant Singh finally left me in the charge of SHO when we reached the table and chairs meant for my inspection purposes. I made brief notes on my observations and impressions based on discussions with SHO (who meekly kept on standing) and after looking into statements and detailed write-up produced by the staff sent in advance.

Inspection over, I made my way to the rest room meant for the Inspecting Officer. Barely had I settled myself to take rest on the sturdy high-level deeply cushioned cot when the great Balwant

Singh, seemingly in his early fifties, reappeared and I had enough time to have a close look at him. His eyes blood shot with traces of opium consumption gleamed with 'Kajal' on the eyelashes. His protruded cheek bones and the sunken cheeks hid his past history of awe-inspiring, cross-border horrific acts of dacoity and murder. His gunshots, it was believed, also struck terror among the poor peasantry of Pakistan as they did on the Indian side. His well-kept long moustache was the only remnant of his awesome past. All told, Balwant Singh with his ornate turban, a Gujrati shirt and a Kutch-style worn dhoti tucked into his loins seemed to be an old specimen of his own well-recognised dacoit character coming out of the pages of pre-1965 (Indo-Pak War) history.

Balwant Singh with his reverential bow and Khamma Ghani invited me to his residence for the evening meal made with Gujarati Rajput menu especially the sweet loaves, 'Roti' made of wheat and barley flour. How to say 'no' with all politeness or to accept in a manner without compromising my official position, this instantly posed a dilemma in my mind. After all, he was still considered the Thikanedar or ex-chief of the area and commanded the respect, which was still reckoned as a historic legacy. The pre-independence Najim of Jodhpur state would have his traditionally accepted, if not mandatory, dinner at Thakur's place without any compunction. But to me, it seemed rather anachronistic besides being against conduct rules to go and dine with an ex-dacoit, however good a gentlemen or special police officer he would have become by then. I overcame my own dilemma by sending for SHO whom I asked to get some food prepared by his staff besides telling the Thakur to send some sweet Gujarati-Kutchi 'Roti' to go with that food. A good sleep lulled and enveloped my shaken nerves.

Next day, early morning, I had left for Barmer before the special police officer, Balwant Singh could return to police station to bid me farewell.

# 12

# Guarding the Gardens

P.K.B. Kurup

After brief spell in a desert district, I assumed charge of a comparatively greener district in the summer of 1974. The dehydrating aridity, the scorching heat and the blinding loo of the desert had created a yearning in me for cool shades and soothing breeze. In the new district, I was happy to see clusters of shady trees lining both sides of the roads. A sanctuary, with an area of over 100 square miles of luxuriant forest growth, lying in the heart of the district provided a pleasing and refreshing sight.

The collectorate was situated on the third floor of an old place from where one could have a commanding view of the surroundings. Within a fortnight of my taking over as the Collector of the district, the Office Superintendent brought a file with a typed order for my signature. When I asked him what it was all about, a routine answer emerged that it was for fixing dates for auctioning some of the gardens in the district. I asked him to leave the file on the table. This did not satisfy him. He cautioned that the government had fixed a final date for carrying out the auction and delay would be taken serious notice of by the government. I pacified him by saying that it was for the first time that the matter had come up before me and that I should have some time to study it. I made it clear to him that I would not sign the order unless I examined and understood its implications in full. When he left the room, I had a rapid glance over the file and discovered that the auction was to be held in pursuance of a high-level decision, as the gardens were a losing concern and a perpetual liability on the government. That night, I went through every page of the file. The government had given approval to the auction of 18 gardens situated in different parts of the district. The picture of devastation came before me, and the orders I was asked to sign appeared to me to be a death warrant. Once auctioned, the trees were sure to be hewn down and the area cut into plots and sold at fancy prices, thus putting an end to the greenery. It became clear to me that these gardens, being permanent assets of the government in reserve, should not be allowed to be frittered away in haste.

## The Sylvan Setting

Next day, on my way to the collectorate, I drove through three or four of these gardens located in the town itself. I saw many children playing in the cool shade, and old men and women moving about. The sylvan setting was enchanting to me. The chirping of the birds, the frolicking of the squirrels and the atmosphere of serenity, which prevailed there, all these cast a spell on me. I felt as though a mute message was being transmitted to me to prevent the inexorable fall of the axe. I got down from the vehicle and talked to some of the children and also to the others who were in the garden. I wanted to know the immediate reaction to the proposal to sell it off in auction. None of them could contemplate the proposal with equanimity. They drew a long face, and some of them were struck dumb. A middle-aged person, who appeared to be informed about the local affairs, blurted out that big money was at the back of it. I got into my vehicle in a pensive mood and reached the office. I told the Office Superintendent that I had studied the case and that I would like to convene a meeting of the district-level officers to chalk out a line of action. I could discern unmistakable approval in his wrinkled face.

## Ascertaining Alternatives

The meeting was convened within a couple of days. The government order was explained to the district-level officers and their views were ascertained. Some of them expressed concern over this order; others advised its early execution. However, a consensus emerged that all the gardens should be inspected by the DLOs, the position studied on the spot, the relevant records collected and, thereafter, have further discussions in a meeting to be convened subsequently.

As the visits were to be undertaken to different places in the district, it was decided to fix the dates in advance. The DLOs, SDOs, *Tehsildars,* concerned ILRs and *Patwaris* assembled at a pre-determined place on the appointed dates and visited all the gardens. The visit to each garden gave an idea of the totality of the problem. We could also informally ascertain the views of the local residents. We discussed the pros and cons then and there and came to tentative conclusions. The land record staff provided the maps of the areas with relevant details. The discussion disclosed that two or three gardens were the subject matter of judicial proceedings. Some gardens were full of mango trees laden with fruit. One or two gardens were found to have the potential for tourist spots. During the hot summer days, all felt that the presence of these gardens was helpful in bringing down the temperature and adding beauty to the whole region. What was required was better management of the gardens rather than throwing away the baby with the bath water. After completing the spot inspection of the gardens located in and about the town, those in the outlying areas were also inspected. Thereafter, a meeting was fixed at the district headquarters to review the findings and propose further action. All the gardens were classified into two broad categories: (a) those which could be looked after by some government departments, and (b) those which were not of specific importance and, therefore, fit for auction.

I prepared a detailed report stating the grounds for retaining most of the gardens and requesting the government to reconsider the decision. This report was finalised after discussing it with the DLOs. It was sent to the Chief Secretary. It was a cyclostyled report and was endorsed to some heads of departments, secretaries to government and DLOs. The proposal contained in the report was to transfer the gardens proposed to be retained to various government departments.

The report was examined at various levels in the secretariat. Some criticised the action of the collector for defying the orders of the government and making a calculated attempt to thwart them. The matter went up to the Finance Minister and the Chief Minister. The highest level appreciated the stand taken by the district administration and, thereafter, the secretariat issued orders virtually accepting the recommendations contained in the report.

The final orders of the government were brought to the notice of the DLOs in a meeting. There was general satisfaction that the hard work put in by the administration in the larger interest of the district had got recognition by the acceptance of the recommendations.

After a few years, I was functioning in the secretariat in the Finance Department. One day, surprisingly enough, a file that dealt with the same matter reached my table. The collector of the district had made a proposal to the government that one of the gardens proposed to be retained by the Revenue Department should be transferred to the municipal board at the district headquarters. I again examined the issue and noted on the file that there was no ground to accept the proposal. My advice was approved at the highest level. Thus, once again, I got the satisfaction that I could make a positive contribution in maintaining the stand taken by the district team of which I had been a member.

# 13

# VVIP Visits

Mohan Mukerji

One of the Secretariat departments directly under the Chief Secretary is GAD (General Administration) and one of the important functions of the GAD is to manage the VIP traffic. The responsibilities became quite onerous when the visitor to the state was a very very important person.

## Presenting a New Look

The President of India came to Jaipur. It was decided that he should see the good work being done in the city to improve living conditions. To the east of the newer part of the city, a large residential complex had been constructed by the Rajasthan Housing Board. It was named Jawahar Nagar. There were houses of six categories, two varieties each for low-, medium- and high-income groups. Originally, there was no constraint on the availability of land since the entire area was mainly unoccupied land owned by the state government, which had been transferred to the Housing Board. Hence, except for the highest category—H/II—where each house was an independent single-storey structure within a compound, all other type designs provided for two adjacent single-storey houses with a common wall. In all cases, there was scope for construction of a similar unit on the first floor, whenever the house owner could himself finance the additional construction in the future. This made the Housing Board houses a good investment.

In later years, of course, as land prices in Jaipur increased rapidly and availability of unoccupied government land dwindled, the Housing Board took to constructing flats in Jawahar Nagar but this stage in development of Jawahar Nagar had not been reached when the President visited Jaipur.

On the other hand, the Housing Board had then taken up the construction of a really low-cost, single-storey house, consisting of one room and a covered verandah, without window shutters, built of simple building blocks made by mixing a bit of cement concrete with broken pieces of stone. Since the regular houses were all built of stone, plenty of stone being quarried for over two centuries from the hills lying to the east of Jaipur, the broken pieces used for these building blocks were really waste material. The house cost was then about ₹ 4,000. It was named Gandhi Griha. The Housing Board won a prize in a Delhi exhibition on low-cost housing.

Much of the credit for the good work done by the Rajasthan Housing Board was due to its first Housing Commissioner who was a civil engineer borrowed from the State PWD (Public Works Department responsible for roads and government housing, offices as well as residences).

(Taken from the author's *Non-Story of a Chief Secretary During Emergency Et Cetera,* New Delhi: Associated, 1982).

Jawahar Nagar was the first large residential area in Jaipur to have a system of sewage disposal. There were conveniently located shopping centres. Skilled artisans previously working as employees of large contractors were encouraged to become small contractors. When the President came to Jaipur, there was a new Housing Commissioner but the first Chairman, a person with a political background, was continuing.

The President was shown a Gandhi Griha, an L-II unit owned by a lady school teacher, and an M-II unit which did not have any owner yet and so was furnished with advice from my wife. There was a well-attended meeting in one of the parks of Jawahar Nagar under a huge colourful *shamiana* (a temporary roof made of cloth supported by bamboo poles).

Like all cities in poor countries, Jaipur has the problem of squatter colonies with extreme slum conditions in the midst of shacks made out of old cloth, mats from reeds and sheets beaten out of tin containers. Sometimes driven out of illegally occupied land, the people occupied some other vacant land. The Rajasthan Government and the Urban Improvement Trust of Jaipur embarked upon a scheme of improving these *kachchi bastis* (temporary colonies). People were persuaded to take down their hutments and build them again in such a way that there could be straight lanes between rows of hutments. These lanes were given street lights and public water taps. Some of the money came from shifting all hutments adjoining main roads and selling the roadside land by auction to those willing to build shops and other commercial accommodation.

The main function during the President's visit was arranged in one of these *kachchi basti* improvement schemes. The response was enthusiastic. The Collector of Jaipur was a colourful personality. The last speech to thank everybody was by him. Fond of literature, he spoke in very high-flown Hindi, which went over the head of many persons present, including me and, perhaps, the President who was a Muslim from Assam. The ladies of Jaipur organised a function in the Ravindra Manch (hall) in the honour of the President's wife. There were other items in that day's programme.

One important job completed during the Emergency, as far as the city of Jaipur was concerned, was the removal of the footpath shops that had come into existence in 1947 when India was partitioned while getting independence and millions of refugees from what is today Pakistan poured into the newly independent India. A new generation grew up, and the erstwhile displaced persons (DPs) became an integral part of the ocean of humanity living in India. A scheme was drawn up for the removal of the footpath stalls and making the DP stall holders shift to a brand new market. This market was built on a strip of land running along the old city walls of the Pink City.

The residents of the strip of land were the poorest of the poor in Jaipur. They and the DP footpath stall holders required much persuasion to move out and make the scheme successful. Sometimes persuasion had to be made more convincing by keeping bulldozers near and trucks to carry away the rickety stalls and household belongings. When the market was completed, the DP leaders named it Indira Bazaar after the Prime Minister. The Vice-President of India came to Jaipur to formally declare the market open. Another VVIP visit.

To honour persons held in respect by many, it is difficult to build new memorials: roads, buildings, institutions such as hospitals, schools and markets. Quite often people wielding authority take the easier path of merely renaming an existing thing. In 1977, the new market was renamed Behari Bazaar. In 1980, the old name of Indira Bazaar was revived. When roads and gardens everywhere were being renamed after persons well known in Indian history and the names of British personages who had also formed part of our history were being removed, somebody suggested that a statue of Queen Victoria should be renamed as Sarojini Naidu statue—in bronze, the matronly figure would evoke respect, whoever it was made to represent.

Irrespective of the name of the new market, it gradually began to attract good business. Persons displaced from the footpaths who had grumbled about the scheme soon found that they had become owners of valuable property without having made any substantial investment in it. Some persons, who had been foolish enough to lose control over their shops by taking in financing partners, had to wait for another opportunity to display their goods on a crowded footpath.

## Unfolding the Past

The VVIP who drew the biggest crowds and caused hard-working officials of the GAD to work their hardest was of course the Prime Minister. During my tenure, the Prime Minister visited Bharatpur, Udaipur and Ajmer. Bharatpur has a wonderful bird sanctuary. An international conference of birdwatchers took place in Bharatpur. To coincide with it, the India Tourism Development Corporation, a Central Public Sector concern, built a beautiful hotel within the bird sanctuary. The Prime Minister came to inaugurate both. Her journey, however, commenced from Deeg where she landed by helicopter. Deeg was the original capital of a very energetic though short-lived dynasty of rulers who were Jat by caste, that is, peasant cultivators in origin, instead of being from the traditional warrior and land-owning caste, the Rajputs. The Jat rulers of Deeg hastened the downfall of tottering Mughal Empire in the eighteenth century. They repeatedly plundered Agra and even Delhi. They soon came in conflict with the growing British power. Deeg and other forts had immensely thick mud walls that did not crumble under British cannon balls. But Jat resistance was finally overcome. The ruling dynasty continued merely as feudatories of the British. Bharatpur became the capital of a princely state of the same name. This state later became a part of the state of Rajasthan formed after India had gained independence. With the addition of the old princely state of Dholpur, Bharatpur became one of the 26 districts of Rajasthan. But Deeg is still the most interesting place. The palace inside the fort has exquisite nineteenth-century European furniture and Indian carpets. In the grounds, there are wonderful pieces of marble work looted from Mughal palaces. The fountains in the formal Mughal style garden are connected with a set of separate water tanks. The tanks were filled in the past by a system of swinging poles that lifted water from one level to another starting from deep wells below the fort walls and ending with the water tanks high up inside the fort; at present, electric pumps are used only if there is a VVIP visitor. In the tanks, dyes of different colour are mixed into the water. When the fountains started to work in honour of the Prime Minister, each jet threw out water of a different colour.

From Deeg the PM went to Bharatpur by road, thousands lining the road for miles. There were functions in Bharatpur mainly next day, but the PM found time to go round the bird sanctuary early in the morning. After the PM's departure, when all those who had gone to Bharatpur on duty began to leave, I accepted the offer of the CM (Chief Minister) to accompany him in the large car in which he was travelling back to Jaipur. In the car, we discussed a few matters. Then there was quiet, and I kept looking out of the window. I spoke something to draw the CM's attention. Not hearing any response, I turned my head. The CM was fast asleep with legs curled upon the seat and the head resting on the edge of the back of the seat. He was making up for lost sleep. I realised that one had to develop many rare personal qualities to become a political leader. I can never sleep in a car.

## Glory of Haldighati

Maharana Pratap is one of the heroes of Indian history. He fought a desperate war throughout his life to maintain the independence of the kingdom of Udaipur (also referred to as Mewar) against the mighty Mughal Empire. The Mughal Emperor was Akbar, one of the greatest rulers in India's history, who won the loyalty and esteem of his people by his policy of showing equal respect to all religions. The Mughal army had a large element of Rajput troops. Raja Man Singh of Amber (the previous capital of the Jaipur state) was the most important and successful general of the Emperor Akbar. The only important Rajput kingdom that still resisted incorporation into the Mughal Empire was Mewar. Man Singh was sent as the head of a large Mughal Army to extinguish the independence of Mewar. The two armies fought at Haldighati. Tactically, Man Singh was successful in drawing the Mewar army out of their easily defendable mountain pass *(ghati)* and inflicting heavy casualties, but Rana Pratap was persuaded by his loyal nobles to leave the battlefield to carry on the war. His beloved horse, Chetak was grievously wounded but carried his master to safety and then died. Man Singh had to return to Delhi with the remnants of his army.

When 400 years came to pass after this historic battle, the Rajasthan Government decided to observe the 400th anniversary of the battle of Haldighati in a big way. The initiative was taken by the Department of Tourism. The Chief Secretary was the Secretary for Tourism as this had always been a part of GAD in the secretariat.

Rajasthan's history is full of stories of bitter rivalry between the various Rajput clans. Poignancy is added to some of the stories because of the Rajput custom of having a bride always from outside one's own clan; many women given away as a bride during temporary peace found their husbands at war with their fathers and brothers. But in today's Rajasthan, these clan rivalries are usually used for joking. The Director of Tourism was from one of the well-known Rajput families of Jaipur. Noticing his enthusiasm for the 400th anniversary celebrations, I asked him, 'Aren't you a Kachhawa (the clan to which the members of the ruling family of Jaipur, the descendants of Raja Man Singh, belonged)? How are you interested in celebrating your ancestor's failure?'

'No, I am not a Kachhawa. And, Sir, the largest number of tourists who visit Haldighati are Bengalis. They all pick up a bit of the soil and put it on their forehead to show that it is sacred to them'.

He was right. Rana Pratap is as much a hero in West Bengal as in Rajasthan. Bengal was the first extensive area to come under British rule. The people were the first to get Western education and develop modern concepts of nationalism. The first anti-British movement began in Bengal. Pitted against the might of the British Empire, the Bengali patriot found his heroes among those who had desperately resisted imperial power in India's history. Rana Pratap was one of them.

Plans were drawn up for the celebrations. A handsome rest house was built at Haldighati where nothing had existed except a simple stone structure which was the tomb of the loyal horse, Chetak. The PWD engineers built the walls of the rest house with the small flat broken stones, which are still used as the common building material in the villages in that area. The sloping roof was made really of reinforced cement concrete, but to make it look like the village roofs it was covered with *kelu* (small hand-made terracotta tiles). Modern toilets were provided. The hall inside, to be used later as a restaurant, had a large map displaying all the important points in the famous battle. The road to Haldighati was little used. It was widened and strengthened to carry the expected future increase in the number of tourists.

The Prime Minister accepted the invitation to address a public meeting at Haldighati. The preparations for the visit took the Chief Minister, other ministers, myself, the IGP (Inspector General of Police) and a number of senior officials to Udaipur. In keeping with Rajasthani traditions of hospitality, it was decided to present the Prime Minister with a gift. A few pieces of Pichhwai paintings were brought from Nathdwara. This place is the seat of the head of an important Vaishnav sect. The paintings were originally used as a background for the images that were worshipped; but for some years, the Pichhwai paintings have become items of interior decorations in homes as well as in hotels. One of the pieces brought for our approval was gorgeous with plenty of gold paint. The Chief Minister liked it. Another piece had no gold in it and had intricate figures of human beings and animals and green trees, all in subdued shades on a dark background. I liked it. I felt that the Prime Minister would appreciate it more than the golden Pichhwai. The IGP agreed with me. The DIG (Intelligence) happened to be present and, whether out of feelings of loyalty to his superior or because of his own aesthetic taste, he too agreed with me.

'I am outvoted', said the Chief Minister.

The Tourism Department prepared a glossy booklet about the battle of Haldighati. There were portraits of the historical personages, printed from beautiful Rajput miniatures. It was an attractive publication. Suddenly, to my horror, I read lines quoted from the English translation of the works of a Mughal historian who was in the Mughal army in that battle. Some Mughal cross-bow men could not distinguish between the Rajput cavalry soldiers in their own army led by Raja Man Singh and in the army of Rana Pratap.

'Shoot your cross-bow arrows at any horseman; one infidel will die whichever army he may be fighting for', was the advice given to the Muslim cross-bow men. The booklet was withdrawn. It would have caused problems. As part of the preparations for the visit of the Prime Minister and the public meeting she was to address, we visited all important sites of the battlefield of 400 years ago. At the spot where the horse, Chetak had died there was an old, simple and small stone structure. I agreed with the officer of the Archaeological Department of the state government that the memorial to Chetak should remain as it was. The Chief Minister agreed with the Chief Engineer that the memorial should be painted up since it was the only historical structure existing at Haldighati. On this issue, I was completely outvoted. This was democracy in administration.

At some distance from Haldighati, we properly saw the fairly flat land which had been the scene of fierce fighting. This area is now well-known for the roses wich grow the blood that had flowed in the battle is said to have made the soil suitable for roses. In one corner, there stood a government school building. Near it were a few tombs. The Rajput Hindu warriors in both the armies who had died in battle had been cremated later. The Mughal army lost some Muslim commanders over whose remains tombs were constructed. There was a Muslim commander in the army of Rana Pratap. One tomb was his.

The great day came. The Prime Minister arrived at Udaipur airport. The crowd broke the police cordon. She addressed a huge crowd in Udaipur city. Helicopters took her, her entourage and some of us to a spot very near to Haldighati. The crowd there was enormous and colourful, with people in bright *lehenga* (wide skirt) and turbans overflowing on to the slopes of the hills around the meeting place. It was too warm for my closed-collar silk suit. All those who had gone by helicopters returned in them. Later I learnt that getting out of Haldighati in cars, buses, scooters and 'bullock carts' was more difficult than managing to survive in the old battle of Haldighati.

### Motorcade at Ajmer

Another visit of the Prime Minister was to Ajmer for a function at Mayo College, an institution established during British days for the benefit of the boys from the families of the ruling princes and feudal landlords but now one of India's best known public schools. There was a large crowd at Jaipur airport where the Prime Minister and her party disembarked from the aircraft and then got into the helicopters to reach Ajmer, which has no landing ground for aircraft. The road from the helipad to the Ajmer stadium was lined with people and still a huge gathering was present at the stadium. After the speeches and cheers, the motorcade arrived at Mayo College where lunch was served at the residence of the principal. The main function was in the afternoon.

I thoroughly enjoyed my part in all these activities. I was Collector of Ajmer twice—it is rarely that an IAS officer holds charge of the same district twice in his career. Meeting old acquaintances was a pleasure. But the most interesting man I met that day was a minister from one of the small but oil-rich Arab countries. Years ago, he had been a student in Mayo College. The Additional IGP of Rajasthan who was in our official team, had been a student in Mayo College when the Arab Minister was also in this institution. They recounted many of their boyhood pranks and we all enjoyed the stories. I later on learnt that the Arab Minister had presented expensive watches to all his school teachers.

The arrangements for visits of the President and the Prime Minister were according to detailed printed instruction books supplied by the central government to all state governments. The motorcade always had a fixed pattern. After the pilot vehicle, came the journalists and photographers; then the vehicle of the VVIP. Next was the vehicle containing the security men and behind that the extra vehicle to be placed in position to carry the VVIP in case his or her vehicle developed any mechanical problem. In a motorcade of this type, as Chief Secretary, I always travelled in a Follow Car, alongwith the IGP and the Home Secretary. I never saw any engine failure in the VVIP vehicle. What drew my admiration was the way in which the security men functioned. The crowds along the route often stopped the VVIP vehicle to present garlands, bouquets or raise aloft in their arms little children to be blessed; and sometimes merely to shout slogans. As soon as the VVIP car stopped, the security men jumped out of their car and surrounded the VVIP car to ensure that no mischievous person takes advantage of the general atmosphere of boisterous enjoyment. As soon as the VVIP car began to move again, the security men would jump back into their car, sometimes already moving. Most of them were, no doubt, agile young men particularly trained for this type of duty but I deeply appreciated the agility and devotion to duty displayed by some very senior middle-aged police officers.

### Sanjay's Sojourn

The Prime Minister's younger son, late Sanjay Gandhi, was then quite prominent politically and very popular as a youth leader. He did not hold any formal office in the central government. He paid a visit to Jaipur. It was easily anticipated that there would be immense crowds and the Chief Minister and other ministers would greet him at the airport and be present at the various functions which he was scheduled to attend. So, most of the arrangements for a VVIP visit had to be made so that the crowds could be controlled. The Chief Secretary and the IGP had to be present but at a discreet distance since the functions were not organised by the state government as such. We had to be near enough to take decisions and give orders if there was any breakdown in the arrangements. The visit went off without any untoward incident. In the procession through the Pink City, the VVIP decided at one point to change from one vehicle to another—the latter was an open jeep. The Chief Minister had the infirmity of being with only one arm, having lost the other in some childhood accident. He had difficulty in quickly getting into the jeep. A Superintendent of Police disguised as one of the thousands of citizens helped the Chief Minister into the moving jeep and with a precarious foothold on a rear bumper held on to the Chief Minister till he could be seated safely.

### McNamara's Visit to Rajasthan Canal

The President of the World Bank was a very different type of VVIP. Instead of preparations for handling large crowds, a lot of homework had to be organised. The visit was to the Rajasthan Canal Project of which Stage I had been completed and work had begun on Stage II. A major controversy existed among technical personnel, non-technical bureaucrats and politicians about what should be the scope of Stage II. The natural flow of water in this area is towards the west, that is, towards Pakistan. The land has very little population. It is full of sand dunes, stable or shifting, large and small. Irrigation can change the entire character of this part of the Thar Desert. In the course of years, it can become a rich agricultural region, like the present irrigated portion of Ganganagar district, which too had been a part of the Thar Desert when the enlightened ruler of Bikaner state, Maharaja Ganga Singh, carried through the Gang Canal project.

To the east of the main canal lie the more settled areas where the existing population live by means of dry land cultivation depending upon slight annual monsoon rains and few deep wells, substantially supplemented by keeping herds of cows, camels, sheep and goats grazing in vast stretches of land unsuitable for cultivation and hence, legally, the property of the state government. There was one school of thought that considerable portion of the water from the main canal could be lifted to high points along the east bank and from these points lift canals could flow into these areas. The technical feasibility of the lift canals scheme was studied by the WAPCOS, a central government public sector consultancy organisation. The report was in favour of lift canals.

Construction of lift canals would mean that there would be less water available for the uninhabited desert areas lying to the west of the main canal. There would be less expenditure on land levelling, road building and establishing new villages and market towns since the total area to be served by flow irrigation would be less. But this also meant that less people could be settled in presently uninhabited land which can be brought under irrigated cultivation.

The pumping of enormous quantities of water into the lift canals would reduce the availability of power for well irrigation in other parts of Rajasthan and for industry. The cost of delivering irrigation water in lift canal areas would be very high due to power costs but it would be difficult, politically, to either charge much higher irrigation rates from those benefiting from the lift canals or to raise the general irrigation rates to recover the higher cost of lift irrigation. As it is, the irrigation rates are artificially low and the income from supply of irrigation water does not even cover the maintenance costs of the various irrigation systems, big and small. This phenomenon is part of the Indian socio-economic system of not making the agriculturist pay the economic price for the inputs supplied by the government or any tax proportionate to his income from land, so that he does not try to raise the price of his produce on these grounds.

Before the visit of the World Bank President, I got together a small team of statisticians and irrigation engineers to work out the various alternatives possible in dividing the available water for Stage II into lift and flow irrigation areas. Approximate construction costs, area development costs, cultivated area, additional population that could be settled and prospects of crop production, all this was worked out in respect of each of the possible combinations of lift and flow irrigation. The size of the problem in Stage II can be appreciated from the fact that the cultivable command area by lift irrigation was estimated to be 2,60,000 hectares (6,50,000 acres) if maximum area was served by lift canals, and the area that could still be irrigated by flow system was estimated to be 5,00,000 hectares (12,50,000 acres).

Although the World Bank President was to visit the Rajasthan Canal Project (RCP) only, it was decided to brief him about the problems of drinking water supply in Rajasthan. This involved more homework.

Robert McNamara, the World Bank President, was scheduled to arrive at the Indian Air Force station at Suratgarh. The previous day, I took the opportunity to see for the first time the archaeological site of Kalibangan; the widespread remains of a Harappan city, with what was considered to be a pre-Harappan area at one corner, formed a wonderful sight indeed. There were pieces of perforated sides of terracotta vessels used apparently to keep eatables, which needed fresh air to preserve them. Among foundations of houses along what had been straight streets there were two skeletons, with their head placed north. The Archaeological Survey of India had a collection of interesting finds but they never had the funds to build a site museum where visitors could see them.

Mr and Mrs McNamara arrived, alongwith some World Bank officials and central government officers. At my suggestion the Rajasthan Small Industries Corporation had got prepared beautiful folders of embroidered camel skin to hold literature on the RCP Stage II and the Drinking Water Scheme. These were presented to the visitors. Helicopters then took us all to one area in the RCP Stage I so that prosperity, which had been caused by the RCP, could be appreciated. The World Bank President moved about among the farmers and asked them many questions. The sun was hot. A bright engineer of the RCP produced umbrellas that had little fans fitted inside, powered by dry cells within the handle.

Helicopters then carried us to a place where construction was in progress on a distributary. The visitors could see that sophisticated machinery as well as camel carts improved by equipping them with pneumatic tyres and even donkeys, was being used. At this site, a small exhibition on the RCP was arranged. One of the central government officers saw the calculation sheet about the various combinations of lift and flow irrigation.

'These people have done their homework very well', remarked one of the visitors showing the calculation sheet to the World Bank President.

Again into helicopters, we reached a helipad near the point where the portion of the main canal that would serve Stage II was being constructed. The entire party got into motor cars and travelled up to the place where huge draglines, crawler tractors and bulldozers were working quite near camel carts and donkeys.

During the helicopter journey along the main canal, the visitors saw the miles of desolate land through which the main canal carried the life-giving water to cluster of greenery formed by the distributaries and filed channels. The enormous size of the project and the amount of good work already done were obvious. The World Bank team seemed to be impressed.

After all the sightseeing, lunch was served under a *shamiana* in one of the RCP colonies housing officers as well as homes of the RCP staff working in that inhospitable area. One of the persons presented to the World Bank President was Ustad Hashimuddin, a master craftsman and miniature painter, then about eighty years of age but still producing lamp shades and goblets of camel skin with intricate decoration in gold paint surrounding detailed miniature paintings. His products were breathtakingly beautiful. He has received a Master Craftsman's award from the President of India. One sample of his workmanship was presented to the World Bank President; the desert did not produce food but it did produce beautiful things. To emphasise the fact that the desert was culturally rich, there was also a short programme of music by the traditional musicians. One of them used a small instrument held in his mouth, which produced a drone in different notes depending upon the pressure of the performer's tongue; it did not produce the seven notes in an octave and could be as old as the ruins of Kalibangan.

The VVIP visit ended when helicopters brought us to Bikaner and the visitors boarded the aircraft for Delhi.

### Runa at Ravindra Manch

Who is a VVIP? Can this term be applied only to those who are politically important or hold the strings of very large purses? Any outstanding personality who draws crowds which require some form of control, is a VIP to a bureaucrat and to the police. This criterion was applicable to Runa Laila, the singer from Bangladesh when she came to Jaipur. I had witnessed her performance when she first came to India and sang in a function sponsored by the Indian Council of Cultural Relations, a body closely linked with the Ministry of External Affairs. I was then Additional Secretary in the Central Ministry of Education and the Department of Culture.

One of the office bearers of a Jaipur cultural organisation said to me: 'Sir, your old contacts with Central Department of Culture should make it easy for you to arrange a programme in Jaipur presenting Runa Laila'.

'She is now the rage in Delhi. If her visit can be managed, you can't have the programme in the Ravindra Manch hall. Too many people, mostly youngsters, will want to hear her'.

'If you kindly tell the Chief Engineer of the PWD, the land behind Ravindra Manch can be cleaned up. There is already a pucca (masonry) platform attached to the Manch that can be used as the stage. We will accommodate the people under *shamianas*'.

I soon got in touch with a person who was involved in staging performances by Runa Laila in Delhi. He asked me to speak to a Joint Secretary in the Ministry of External Affairs. Within a day or two, I learnt that Runa Laila would come to Jaipur. As a gesture from our side it was agreed that during their visit to Jaipur, arrangements would be made for her and her mother to pay a visit to the Dargah of Khwaja Moinuddin Chishti in Ajmer, a place of pilgrimage for Muslims of the Indian subcontinent and of Malaysia, as well as for some non-Muslims.

The performance was a grand success. Under the *shamiana*, there were over 3,000 persons. I knew that thousands more would like to listen and so loudspeakers were installed at various points in the Ram Niwas Bagh (garden) where the Ravindra Manch is located. Another 3,000 or so persons heard the songs by grouping themselves near the loudspeakers. There was thus no attempt to break through the flimsy barriers near the *shamiana*.

Runa Laila had an attractive stage presence and a vivacious soulful way of singing. Her repertoire included songs in Urdu, Bengali, Punjabi and Sindhi. One consequence of this performance was that plans were later prepared to convert the open space behind the Ravindra Manch into an open air theatre with capacity to seat about 3,000 people; the stage being adjacent to the Manch building, the green rooms and other facilities of the Manch could be used. About two years after my retirement, I attended the first function in this open air theatre—a day-time conference of engineers.

# 14

# The Elephant and I

**Krishna Bhatnagar**

One bright sunny afternoon during my posting as Collector, Ajmer, I had decided to go and inspect a flower-making training camp being held near the picturesque lake of Foy Sagar. I had barely entered the exhibition room and was admiring the profusion of exotic flowers made of silk, paper and various other materials, when my driver came in to tell me that the SP (Superintendent of Police) had sent a message on wireless that he wanted me to return to my office immediately because an elephant was creating a serious law and order problem in the city.

As there was no telephone in the vicinity, I left the camp for my office. On the way, I wondered why the District SP, who was one of the highest decorated police officers in India with the President's Medal for bravery and Padma Shri thrown in for good measure, wanted me to deal with an elephant. The SP was in any case known for chasing dacoits and not elephants. Even if the dacoits had formed an elephant gang, it was not my domain but his to catch the thieves.

I was almost convinced that the operator had mixed up the message, but when I returned to my office I found a discussion in progress on the law for dealing with mad elephants. I was informed in all seriousness that only after getting a certificate from the Veterinary Doctor that the elephant was insane and a danger to humanity, it would be possible to shoot the elephant. I was too intrigued by the idea to inquire how exactly the examination of the mind of the elephant was to be conducted in a busy street and who among us was to bell the cat (elephant in this case).

Leaving the office people to discuss this very important question, I found out the location of the SP on wireless and left for the site, giving instructions that they first find out whether there was any gun available for either making the elephant unconscious or shooting it. If so, the gun and the person who was capable of handling it should be sent by jeep to the site. If there was no such weapon or person readily available, we should be informed by wireless as early as possible.

I reached the busy street to find the elephant walking straight at a leisurely pace. The SP came to join me in my car duly armed with a fierce looking gun in his hand. He told me that the elephant had gone berserk and was expressing his displeasure by intermittently breaking up whatever he disliked. As if to belie this statement, the elephant for the present was ignoring the crowds and everything else around it and walking or standing leisurely in the middle of the road.

The location of the elephant was on the busiest street of the city. This street functions as the main artery of the town with the railway station situated on one side and shops located on both sides. This road even in normal hours groans with traffic ranging from buses to cars, cycles, tempos, *thelas* and the symbol of Ajmer, tongas.

We decided that as the area was very crowded with shops on both sides and a huge sea of humanity was gathering, it would be a disaster to try shooting the elephant there. We would control the crowd and keep it far from the reach of the elephant.

The crowd in the meantime was straining to get as near as possible, their curiosity getting the better of discretion. The children were fascinated by the display given earlier and kept shouting to the elephant to give them a repeat performance. I was yet to get a first-hand glimpse of the elephant's ringside performance.

### The Rampage

In the meantime, the elephant, which was like any other elephant with four legs, a trunk and a tail, had been walking along slowly with his majestic gait. For no reason, he suddenly stopped and stood near a letter box, outside the general post office. Probably because he found the red colour or the absence of a letter for him offensive, he uprooted it and threw it on one side and continued walking on, as the crowd cheered and clapped at this performance.

After walking a few steps ahead, he found a Matador van belonging to a local girl's school. The elephant decided that he did not like the Matador; so, without the least indication of strain, overturn it. Not being satisfied with this, he proceeded to ram it and trample it with his feet. To the elephant the Matador seemed to be a toy especially created for him to vent his anger. The crowd greeted this performance with enthusiasm and made it clear that they considered the Magistrates and Police who were keeping them from getting nearer as spoil sports.

Getting tired of the Matador, the elephant decided to walk on as if there was no other thought in his mind. After walking about half a mile at a leisurely pace, the elephant took a dislike to a scooter and proceeded to overturn it. After that, he continued to walk across the area of the railway station, stopping occasionally to overturn a cycle here and there.

After walking about a kilometre, the elephant spotted a *thela.* The elephant stood near the *thela* contemplating it with his trunk swinging from side to side. Along with the crowd, we waited with baited breath till he decided that he would not overturn the *thela* but would scatter the papers being carried in it, which he proceeded to do.

## Pied Piper or God?

By this time as far as I was concerned, the incident had stopped being even remotely funny. The elephant was turning into the 'pied piper' of the city. I watched the crowd with more and more anxiety, which seemed to be coming from all directions. The people kept coming from everywhere on foot and on cycles. Those on tongas also directed the tongaman to join the crowd. Some of them suggested that the elephant was connected with God, and they should be allowed to offer him some garlands and fruits. We were not convinced and strengthened the cordon around our VVIP even further.

The elephant continued to walk in the crowded streets. More and more crowds were pouring in from all the sides. My heart missed a beat when a child dashed through the cordon and had to be grabbed by the policemen on duty. I heaved a sigh of relief when the elephant left the crowded streets and came on a wider road. I was wondering where he intended to go because the road ahead would lead to an open area. The crowd did not seem inclined to go back and continued to follow the elephant cheering loudly whenever he overturned a cycle or a scooter.

The elephant tired of his sport walked on ignoring everyone completely. Suddenly I found the elephant leaving the road for a vast open area. He came and stood there looking around peacefully. On his arrival, some *sadhus* who had been sitting nearby came to him and patted his trunk.

The SP and I watched the performance along with the crowd, which stood around. We asked the *sadhus* whether the elephant was part of their entourage. The *sadhus* very happily informed us that the elephant was part of their *toli*, and they were on a *Bharat Darshan*. When we informed the chief *sadhu* of the historic march of the elephant through the town, the *sadhu* registered surprise. He gave a bewildered look at the huge crowd, at us and at the elephant. He said that the elephant had left with his *mahavat*. They had been going to the city for the last three days without any incident.

It took great restraint on my part not to tell him what I thought about him and the elephant turning the town upside down and leading the administration to a merry dance. When the *sadhu* took a second look at the crowd with cycles in their hands, the tongas and scooters, he realised that the elephant had indeed been creating trouble in the city. In defence, he launched into a eulogy in praise of the elephant and tried to convince us that there was no sweeter elephant to be seen throughout the length and breadth of the country. This elephant in its constant travels had brought nothing but goodwill wherever he went.

### A Curious Docility

When we asked him to explain how such a sweet elephant could treat the city as a circus ground, his explanation was that during the past few days he had been observing people in the town throwing coconuts at the elephant as offerings. The elephant had entertained them by catching these in mid-air. This must have happened again. While trying to catch the coconut, the trunk of the elephant may have touched the electric wire giving him a nasty shock. This alone could have provoked this outburst as the *sadhu* was quite convinced that the elephant was a firm believer in peace, and service was his motto. If he had dropped the *mahavat* on the way and walked through the town alone, it was only because he must have been given immense pain.

I was wondering by this time if it was the same elephant we were talking about. After having followed it down the streets I was in no mood to swallow such tales, so I requested the *sadhu* to prove the elephant's innocence. He promptly agreed and told me to relay commands for him. I asked that the elephant be made to do *uthak bethak* five times. The elephant obeyed every command promptly. After that, on further instruction he saluted the crowd on all sides with his trunk. He was even willing to stand on three legs and salute them. I was satisfied that the earlier performance in the streets was a stray incident. Feeling extremely relieved that the whole episode had passed away without damage to human life, we decided to let the matter rest. We told the *sadhus* to move out of the city within one hour with their elephant, under police escort.

By the evening, the news had spread with *namak masala* all over the city. At a party, friends had a field day discussing whether the elephant being a male chauvinist had gone berserk on hearing that there was a lady Collector posted in the town; whether he had first gone berserk and then stopped his performance after having turned round and seen a lady officer with a gun following him.

# 15

# The Floods

R.S. Kumat

It was *kawwali* night. On the occasion of Urs Fair in Ajmer, held in the memory of Sufi Saint Khwaja Moinuddin Chishti, *kawwals* (devotional singers) come from near and far places and sing *kawwalis* in the Dargah (the religious place where the tomb of Khwaja Moinuddin Chishti lies). They also hold public and private sessions. The district administration had arranged a public function of *kawwali* on the evening of 17 July 1976, and famous *kawwals* gave their performance almost throughout the night. In the early hours of 18 July, after the *kawwali* programme was over, the SP (Superintendent of Police) and I took a round of the Dargah Bazar where the mass Friday prayer would take place next morning to look at the arrangements and ensure that everything was set for the next day. At about 5 o'clock in the morning, I went to bed and just after two hours got up to see that it had started raining. It was the month of rains, and it was not unusual to have rains. Normally such rains last for about an hour or so and as the rains started, one hoped that the temperature would cool down and weather would become fine for the *namaz* (mass prayer), which would take place at 2.00 p.m. However, the rains did not stop; on the contrary, the intensity increased and by about 10 o'clock a number of phone calls started coming in with a message that certain low-lying areas had been flooded and there was lot of water everywhere. The number of telephone calls started going up and even before I could organise the relief parties, the phone went out of order. I tried to contact the SP through wireless, only to know that even his house had been flooded. Other staff could not move out because of rains and whoever had tried to take out his vehicle, got stuck in the waters gushing through the roads.

## Communicational Impediments

Realising that contact through phone or wireless was not possible, I moved out myself in a jeep, but even the jeep could not negotiate through the flood waters on the road. Hence, I got down and looked for a heavy vehicle. A truck passed through that side and I asked its driver to take me to the telephone exchange. Moving in this truck and negotiating my way to the telephone exchange, I realised the immensity of the situation and therefore contacted army authorities and state headquarters to seek help. It, however, came to notice later that no help from outside was possible because the road and rail communications had been damaged and no vehicular traffic could come to Ajmer except from Jaipur side.

Having contacted the state capital, I went to the Ana Sagar, the historic lake of Ajmer where from emerges the Luni river, carrier of large quantities of water through the desert and ending in the Rann of Kutch. Not surprisingly, Luni was overflowing and all its surplus water was moving through a small *nala* across the city. The capacity of the *nala* had been greatly reduced as a result of population pressure and lack of annual cleaning arrangements. The original size of the *nala* had been reduced by making it a *pucca nala* and the area so reclaimed was used for developing colonies. This *nala* was good enough to carry only the normal sewage, and not the flood waters, which were unprecedented.

## The Devastating Downpour

In the living memory of the people, this was the first ever flood Ajmer had experienced and the main reason was the downpour of about 275 mm (11 inches) in three hours between 7.00 a.m. and 10.00 a.m., whereas the averaged annual rainfall for the city was only 350 mm (14 inches). It naturally meant that at any time the normal precipitation would not be more than 50–75 mm (2–3 inches), and the *nala* was sufficient to carry that much water. But the precipitation was so intense that no drain could carry this amount of water. On the one hand, the rainfall had not yet stopped and on the other hand, the Ana Sagar was releasing as much as 3,000 cusecs of water. All the colonies that had been constructed in the downstream of the *nala* experienced heavy flood and people had 5–6 feet of water in their houses and all their belongings were either swept away or damaged and *katcha* houses were completely washed away. Immediate need was to rescue the people and take them to safe shelters.

Normal population of Ajmer at that time was around 3.5 lakh, and it increased then by about another 2 lakh as a result of pilgrims coming for the Urs, from all over India and neighbouring countries such as Pakistan. The Dargah of Khwaja Moinuddin Chishti is located in a most congested place right at the foothill of the Taragarh Fort, the towering feature of Ajmer as a part of the Aravallis. It is difficult to accommodate this increased population in that area. Almost all the pilgrims who come by rail make their own stay arrangement, but those who come by chartered buses, have to be provided with a parking place and other sanitary facilities. Ajmer is surrounded from all sides by hills and as such the nearest place that the administration could locate was on the banks of the Ana Sagar. In the previous ten years, Ana Sagar never got filled to its capacity and no wonder, the upper reaches of the Sagar were considered as a safe place for parking and provision of camp facilities for the pilgrims. This place, popularly known as Vishram Sthal had more than 400 buses parked in this area and the pilgrims would normally keep their belongings in the buses and sleep in the shelters near and around it, while during the day, they went to the Dargah for paying their homage. Fortunately, the rains took place in the morning and so almost all pilgrims had left the buses for safe places apprehending the danger of increased waters in the lake, but the buses could not move out and about 100 buses got drowned in the flooded Ana Sagar. Thus, the emergency for rescue and relief had been created both for the normal population living in the town and in the downstream of the *nala* and for the pilgrims in Vishram Sthal. In the Dargah Bazar area, water coming from the hills passes through the Nala Bazar (the original *nala* or drain for carrying flood waters had become a bazar and so named as Nala Bazar) and as the velocity was very high, some people were swept away. The local people however rescued them through ropes, etc.

At Vishram Sthal, the buses had been drowned, but there was no casualty and all the people had taken shelter in the upper reaches of the Vishram Sthal. The bus owners had engaged some trucks to pull the buses out of waters. This of course was a matter that could take time and accordingly I decided to leave that spot and go to the area in the downstream of the *nala* carrying the surplus water of Ana Sagar. On the way, I met the Additional SP and ADM (Additional District Magistrate). They were trying to do whatever little they could on their own, but the organised effort could not be started because of the lack of communications. Only by about 12.00 noon, we got organised and take a round of the area. The most affected area was a slum known as Jadugar Basti. Most of *its* inhabitants were employees of the railway workshop. Their houses and belongings had been completely washed away, but fortunately there was no casualty in this *basti.* Later, as we took stock of the casualty situation, we found that only three persons had died as a result of being swept away in a *nala* or due to house collapse. The major problem was the provision of shelter and food.

## Managing Relief through Concerted Action

Finding that the area of operation was near Jadugar Basti, we all operated from the office of Ajanta Cinema, which was the nearest point from the *basti* and the only place where we got a telephone in working order. Parties were sent to different areas for reconnaissance and provision for food. We purchased some dry ration and got it distributed. The local inhabitants had also prepared food and brought for distribution to the flood affected families. Soon they found that whatever they had brought was precious little and hence were being mobbed. It was also evident that people were distributing food items time and again in certain areas, while in some other areas none of these people had visited. We, therefore, decided to coordinate all the private relief efforts and asked all the people to bring their food articles to a central place from where they would be directed by the district administration for distribution. In all, about 25,000 people had been affected and so nearby schools, *dharamshalas* and some houses constructed by the Rajasthan Housing Board were occupied. Besides, kitchens were opened for preparing food.

On 18 July, we could only distribute dry ration, coordinate activities of the voluntary agencies and provide immediate shelter. Other necessary measures such as disconnecting of power, lest there should be short-circuiting and cases of electrocution, and deployment of police force to keep a watch throughout the night, were taken. Moreover, full-scale measures were planned from the morning of 19 July onwards.

On the second day, we shifted our office to the nearest railway building, which was normally used for arranging club activities, and opened our camp office for relief operations. The City Magistrate was made in charge of the entire affair, and all voluntary agencies and philanthropic groups were requested not to distribute any article directly to the people. They were asked to either deposit the articles if these were in small quantity or distribute them under the guidance and supervision of the district administration. This was done mainly to avoid overlapping and confusion. The voluntary agencies also felt happy that they were able to reach the needy areas and their effort was not being wasted.

We opened government kitchens in different localities. However, we found to our dismay that the flood-affected families were coming to the kitchen only to receive ready-made food, and the kitchen managers were finding it difficult to feed more than 2,000 persons at a time. The flood-affected people were requested to help in preparing the food, but they declined to help for they did not consider it as a part of their duty; instead, in their view the government was duty-bound to provide everything. I took a round of the kitchens and found that the flood-affected people were sitting and waiting for the food as if they were the guests and were complaining whenever they did not get the food in time. I had no alternative but to ask them firmly and politely to provide help in cooking or else they would not get the food. Some people refused and even tried to question my decision, but persuasion and arousing of their self-respect helped ease the situation. I exhorted them not to rely on charity and instead earn their bread in this calamity by joining hands. A direct talk with the people helped the situation, and we could manage the kitchens without employing extra labour. This arrangement continued for about a week and then we put the people on their own and withdrew the relief arrangements gradually. They needed help in providing clothing, utensils, food and shelter. All this had to be planned quickly and the administration had to normalise the situation so that the people did not remain on charity for long.

The response of philanthropic institutions was substantial, and we received donations in cash and kind from all quarters. The donations in kind were not kept in government store. We encouraged the voluntary agencies to distribute the articles with their own hands under our supervision. This promoted motivation and confidence among the voluntary agencies for they could see that whatever had been donated by them was reaching the needy hands and was not being stored in the government stores. Full lists of affected families with no assistance provided by each voluntary agency helped us to ensure equitable distribution of articles.

The government assistance was limited to food ration, some cash and temporary shelter. There was no provision for clothing, utensils, blankets, etc. This could be done only through voluntary agencies, and it came in good measure. This was further fully proved in the unprecedented floods of Jaipur in 1981. I had the opportunity of organising voluntary effort in that critical situation as well and the experience of Ajmer stood in good stead. Tremendous response of voluntary agencies was responsible for providing permanent shelter, rehabilitation and reclamation of flooded agricultural land. This could not have been achieved by mere government effort.

## Arranging Rehabilitation

Timely relief was not enough and steps were needed for permanent rehabilitation. An assurance against repetition of similar calamity was called for, as unfounded rumours three days after floods created panic and all began to run for safe places. The basic problem of the flood-affected victims was that they were living in *katcha* houses and could not have permanent houses for various reasons, namely, (a) land on which they were squatting was not their own, (b) it was too congested to accommodate all of them, and yet none of them wanted to move out of that area, (c) lack of finance in low-income groups, and (d) reluctance even to replan and regroup the houses in the existing locality. This had been experienced even when the programme of slum improvement was launched much before floods and the inhabitants were asked to have a replanned locality.

Floods enabled us to acquire some additional land and replace the old sites. Effort was made to adjust all the affected people in the same locality by giving each family 50 sq yards plots. Finance for making *pucca* houses was obtained from Life Insurance Corporation, and the Urban Improvement Trust was involved in providing all the necessary facilities such as road, drains, water and electricity. Plans were prepared after consultation with the inhabitants, and the development of the *bastis* was initiated. This was not a small effort by any means because even one person in the locality could hinder the entire development. Besides persuasion, use of local leaders was made to expedite the work and the recalcitrants were dealt with sternly. This resulted not only in rehabilitation, but also in the improvement of slum areas. Six months earlier, efforts made to replan the houses in these very slums had failed, but the floods provided a blessing in disguise and facilitated us to replan the houses in the slums. The experience gained here was used later in replanning the *katchi bastis* of Jaipur.

## The Moral

The story of handling this calamity holds out some important lessons, which can be summarised as follows:

(1) When communications fail in a crisis situation, it is better to move out and collect all those who are available for organising the effort.

(2) Governmental resources are not enough to handle a calamity and therefore voluntary support should be encouraged and properly directed.

(3) Keeping up the morale of affected families during the crisis is a requisite to effective handling of a crisis.

(4) Calamities bring blessings in disguise and one should always see the opportunity to seize the challenge.

The District Collector has multifarious duties and is expected to do everything under the Sun but his office attains crucial importance in times of crisis. It is a great challenge and a time of real test of leadership. It is not a routine job, nor are there precedents or blue books to tackle crises. One has to rely on one's own resourcefulness, but more than that on cooperation from colleagues, political leaders and people at large. The test of leadership lies in the measure of cooperation the Collector can obtain from the various sections of society.

# 16

# From Bondage to Freedom

I.S. Kavadia

I was not only mentally agitated but rather in tears by the time I reached the dak bungalow in the remote area of Shahabad by well past mid-night. The tears in my eyes were in the nature of penance for the atrocities committed by vested interests all through the decades on the most backward and exploited tribals known as 'Saharias' in the state of Rajasthan. Mental agitation was in terms of alternatives open to me for meeting the challenge of beginning an end of this savagery whereby these tribals had all along been treated like chattel without the least expected norms of human sympathy, which would normally be available even to animals.

## The Face of Misery

Throughout the day after leaving headquarters in the early hours of morning, I had been meeting the tribals in the area of my visit—Shahabad Panchayat Samiti in the district of Kota, which is the remotest part of the district beyond the river Parvati and surrounded by Madhya Pradesh on three sides and connected with the headquarters by a bumpy road of approximately 120 km in length, which is crossed by a number of prominent rivers like Kali, Sindh and Parvati, which were luckily not in floods at that time or otherwise I would not even have been able to enter the area beyond

Parvati. During the day, I had covered a number of tribal villages both in Upareti, that is, the upper plateau, and in Taleti, the low-lying area around proper Shahabad, which is the tehsil as well as Panchayat Samiti headquarters. It was no wonder that the town was even without the basic amenity of electricity because of the total number of 435 villages in an area spread over 2,898 sq km, only one village of Kishanganj adjoining Baran Tehsil had this privilege. The area had excess of rain but drinking water was an acute problem so much that in some of the villages, water had to be fetched from a distance as long as 11–13 km, that too after going down about 150–160 m of deep slope leading to river bed. Therefore, the stories of women weeping on breaking of their earthen pots containing water while going up from the river bed were known, because the very idea of going back to village for replacement and facing the ordeal once again was a frightening one.

The sulky men and women I had met were dark in complexion on which if anything was visible that was their penury and misery coupled with the shock of unexpected meeting with the District Collector in their own huts and villages; for so far the very sight of civilised persons had been enough to scare them away into their scheduled hutments deep into this forest belt where they are said to have settled over a 1,000 years ago when they were driven out of their ancestral home, south of the Aravalli ranges beyond Banswara and Dungarpur areas in south Rajasthan—districts which I had served earlier. As they took refuge (*sahara*) in forest, they came to be called Saharias. Originally, they are Bhils and still possess many common features with them. However, I found the Saharias to be rather sullen in nature, obviously due to their excessive exploitation over the centuries—which increased to a considerable extent during the recent past due to construction of inroads by the outsiders, who are bent upon monopolising the best available agricultural lands and in the process not only depriving the tribals of their lands but also converting them into bonded labourers for whom life meant only human suffering and treacherous discomfitures as any of them could be bought or sold like chattel. Having no modicum of support for farming, they largely thrived on barks of trees and fruit of Mahua trees in an area where forest growth was exuberant. The neglect of their environment through centuries kept them completely isolated from the civilised world. That must have been a happy state of affairs, for the later contact with civilisation not only deprived them of whatever they had but also forced slavery upon them.

## The Will to Articulate

I had earlier remained in this district in a junior capacity and therefore knew something about this exploitation. However, what I saw with my own eyes during that day was beyond all possible imagination. I had left the headquarters, on that day soon after joining as the District Collector, with a view to settle some of the problems of Saharias on-the-spot, which I had in my mind on the basis of my prior knowledge and some of the files which had come to my notice during the first few days of my working as the Collector in the district. However, by the time I reached the dak bungalow, I was full of doubts as to the possibility of tackling the situation where the problem was not that of emancipation of poor tribals but of fighting the vested interests at all levels. There were government officials who had connived with influential citizens in not only getting the lands allotted to them but also getting the lands belonging to tribals transferred to them in contravention of law. A number of these government officials also got the lands allotted to their relatives including their wives and children. There were public men who had not only indulged in this but also in other forms of exploitation including usury and keeping the downtrodden tribals as bonded labourers.

The group of tribals who met me in the dak bungalow soon after my arrival there kept on crying, for they had no courage to unburden themselves in the presence of local influential men. These influential local men wanted to nip in the bud the challenge to their traditional hold on the tribals, now threatened on account of the interest being shown by me and my team in the welfare of these tribals. That day the tribals, who otherwise had never dared in the past to meet anybody in authority, had turned out in great number throughout the area to meet me. Naturally, the vested interests did not want tribals to be given an opportunity to speak to me and my team, and they therefore started narrating to me their own sacrifices in terms of loans without material security and consequential losses in terms of bad debts and the various other ways in which they had been helping the tribals and in spite of that, if tribals continued to remain backward how could the same be helped!

## Sagas of Serfdom

Since arguments were not going to help in such a situation. I retired to my bedroom in the dak bungalow and called a few trusted officials who had accompanied me in the day alongwith some social workers from Adim Jati Sevak Samaj Sangh working in the area with whom I had discussed the problems earlier before embarking upon this visit for on the spot study. With their help, it was thought to properly confront the influential persons with specific instances of exploitation narrated by the tribals. If narration of exploitation suffered by these poor tribals was so horrifying, then what must have been its actual experience!

How could one withstand the case of Pema and his 20 colleagues who were fined a sum of ₹ 200 each for cultivating the state forest land in an unauthorised way, although they had been asked to cultivate as share croppers the 120 bighas of land under question by the brother of local Upsarpanch who claimed the land to be his own, and out of 400 bags of wheat grown by them they had been given 20 bags only, i.e., one bag per head? Obviously in such an arrangement which had been in practice for long, the benefits accrued to the cunning ones and Saharias were left only to suffer the consequences. It was only by chance that none of them was imprisoned, otherwise what would have happened to their respective families? In any case, even now they were facing the hardship for they had nothing with them, not to mention about the payment of fine at the rate of ₹ 200 each.

Next was the case of Amya who was advanced a loan of ₹ 2,847 in Samvat year 2026 (June 1969), and it was forced upon him that for repayment of loan he would have to work up to Samvat 2036 (1979). In this particular case as time passed, not only had the son of the bonded labourer been forced to work for the creditor but four *bighas* of his own land was also grabbed by the creditor. Amya, a *hali* (plough man), had made the contract to work for ten years to repay the said advance of ₹ 2,847 along with the condition that he would receive yearly 12 maunds (5 quintals) of barley and a sum of ₹ 10. The cost of barley consumed by the *hali* in excess of 12 maunds as prescribed was recoverable from the *hali*. The most interesting point to note is that up to the year Samvat 2031 (1974), the *hali* could pay only ₹ 285 × 5 = ₹ 1,425. By that time he was, however, having another debt to the same moneylender of ₹ 837 as cost of the barley consumed in excess of the contracted quantity. Let us look at the problem from another angle by converting barley into money terms. The highest price of barley during all those years was not more than one and a half rupee per seer (about 1 kg) and as such total maximum amount the *hali* got in a year was ₹ 720 only as against a minimum wage of four and a half rupee a day, i.e., ₹ 1,642.50 per annum. For the first year, the interest rate comes out to be 22.22 per cent. For the next year, the same amount of interest accrued on ₹ 2,562 giving interest rate of 28.9 per cent. For the third year, the moneylender got interest at the rate of 32.5 per cent. Hence, it was impossible for a bonded labourer to repay his debt.

The case of Pyara, a cobbler of Shahabad, turned out to be even more serious as he was facing a recovery of ₹ 1,500 against his name in the cooperative society whereas as per his statement he never took the said loan. On further enquiry, it turned out that his membership fee of the society was paid by the Sarpanch of Nomera Panchayat who drew the amount on behalf of Pyara fraudulently and pocketed the same. In another case, a tribal mortgaged his pair of bullocks with a moneylender for a sum of ₹ 300, which was duly repaid by the loanee alongwith the interest. But when it came to the bullocks, the moneylender flatly refused to return the same. Meanwhile he arranged the affairs in such a way with the Sarpanch of the Gram Panchayat that the pair of bullocks had been deposited in the cattle pound of the Panchayat on some flimsy and untenable grounds. Later on the moneylender himself purchased the bullocks at a ridiculously low price on the basis of some auction papers which were duly manipulated, and of course, by passing some money in the process to the Sarpanch.

For Parbhu, his marriage became a curse because apart from being domesticated in the process, he not only found himself but also his wife in perpetual bondage from that very day. He had taken a loan of ₹ 500 for the marriage. As per the terms of his agreement, he mortgaged the nose ring and other miscellaneous jewellery valued at ₹ 750 with the moneylender immediately after the arrival of his wife. But even after twenty years, the day after he first met me, he found himself in the worst form of slavery.

## Contemplating an Action Strategy

After taking leave of exploiters as well as the exploited ones in the early hours of morning, and after having assured them to attend to all these matters the next day, I just could not sleep. However, in the course of my tour that day I had successfully exploded the myth, given currency by the vested interests all these years that it was impossible to make these tribals prone to progress, as they preferred to hide inside the jungles at the very sight of the authorities, rather than seeking relief against exploitation. It was now the turn of the authorities to reciprocate, especially when, in spite of all past indifference on their part, tribals had still reposed confidence in them as was evident from the large number in which they had turned out during the day to meet me, notwithstanding all possible threats to them by their exploiters who even till that day appeared to be having sufficient backing of public men and government officials down the line. In the scanty lantern-lit bedroom of the dak bungalow, I kept on pondering about the different aspects of the problem and the ways of tackling it, including the problem of rehabilitation of the tribals who were to be released from this bondage. The problem of stiff opposition from the vested interests had also to be taken care of. A much bigger team of dedicated workers consisting both of officials and non-officials was a must for attending to the work at the desired speed. The local complications posed a continuous procession of problems and in spite of all the legal safeguards in favour of scheduled castes and tribes, no way could be found by which the work could be expedited. In this way, the early hours passed till the rising of the sun when the thought of using powers consequent upon the declaration of Emergency in the country alongwith the normal law came to my mind and a resultant smile on the face notwithstanding the past 24 tiring hours.

### A Quiet Revolution

There was no time left for further thinking in the matter as by the time I could get ready, I found the rest house surrounded by a mammoth gathering of tribals—men, women and children—who easily outnumbered their exploiters who had also gathered there in sufficient numbers. The team of officials, which was deputed for examining on-the-spot cases with the help of the official records and dedicated local social workers of Adim Jati Sevak Samaj Sangh, was ready with factual information in some of the cases. This opportunity appeared to be a right one for me to mobilise the tribals by addressing them and making them aware of their rights and privileges especially after promulgation of the 20-Point Programme of the Prime Minister. Besides, through this process, the exploiters could also be educated discretely and be given hints of the consequences of not falling in line with the changing socio-economic climate. And, by the time my speech had ended, a revolution appeared to have commenced as Amya got not only his land but also freedom; Parbhu and his wife got their ornaments and their freedom; one tribal got back his bullocks; Pema and his 20 colleagues were freed from their mental worry as the brother of Upsarpanch agreed to meet all the liabilities on account of fine which had been imposed on the tribals and the like. A sense of guilt and remorse had obviously overtaken the exploiters concerned but what about thousands of other such cases? Could all the exploiters or at least a majority of them be made to behave accordingly in the cases to which they were a party? Obviously not, because many of them had made it clear to me there itself of their intentions of not budging in the matter. And naturally so when they were sure of necessary support from the right quarters, as and when required, to which they had all along been accustomed and especially when some of these influential ones had been right there with me in the course of my tour about which I appeared to be unaware of. Fortunately, however, I was not totally ignorant of these black sheep, though I feigned ignorance on my part as a necessary concomitant of overall strategy because it was not at all possible to open all the fronts simultaneously, particularly when the presence of a few members of the vested interest groups with me also proved helpful to a considerable extent in achieving the objectives as it gave the impression that these persons were also supporting the programme and this helped in reducing resistance on the part of the exploiters, at least at the outset.

## Sketching the Stratagem

Since time was the essence of the whole problem, exact identification of the issues involved was just not possible, and therefore, relying on hurried visits to the area by the officials and innumerable discussions and interviews with the tribals, the following objectives were laid down before the official machinery which was expected to work with public support:

1. Restoration of illegally grabbed land to the rightful tribals or in case such land happened to be government lands, restoration of the same to the state for allotment to tribals or other weaker sections, unless it happened to be forest land and not thought proper whether to be allotted for agricultural purposes.
2. Identification and release of bonded labourers.
3. Liquidation of rural indebtedness with priority to cases involving human exploitation.
4. Ensuring minimum agriculture wages.
5. Institutional arrangements for providing agricultural inputs and financing thereof, *ex gratia* relief to tribals pending arrangements for alternative employment, employment of all the educated tribals who are found suitable in various departments, of government and elsewhere.
6. Long-term proposals for the development of the area, including expansion of facilities such as roads, irrigation and electricity.

However, the cases of alienation of land from tribals to non-tribals and their exploitation by way of indebtedness and bondage were always not separable in practice, since all indebtedness these three elements had gone hand in hand.

With the declaration of Emergency and enunciation of 20-Point Programme by the Prime Minister, though awakening had come to masses, by and large, these poor people in the remote area of Shahabad were hardly aware of the same, and wherever some signs of the same were visible, the heavy hand of exploiters was enough to silence them. The discussions at higher political and administrative levels proved to be of immense value in chalking out further strategy for achieving desired results within the shortest possible time. Every possible care had to be taken because the exploiters who had contravened all possible laws in the process of exploiting the poor and ignorant tribals had the right to resort to law when it suited them, more so when they had necessary finances accrued to them in the past from the exploitation which could legitimately be used by them for fighting its perpetuation.

The Rajasthan Tenancy Act, vide Section 42, had provided for nullity of a sale, gift or bequest by *khatedar* tenant of his interest in the whole or part of his holding if such sale, gift or bequest happened to be by a member of scheduled tribe in favour of a person other than scheduled tribes. However, all along, this provision had been honoured in breach rather than in observance—of course, in connivance with public or government functionaries at various levels. Similarly, land alienation by tribals to non-tribals by way of mortgage had been restricted vide Section 43 of the same act, but prospectively only. Sub-clause (2) of Section 43, which came into force in 1970, had laid down a maximum period of mortgage up to ten years but in the year 1976 the usufructuary mortgage contracted during the period 1966–1976 could not have been satisfactory. By an amendment in 1975, maximum mortgage period had however been restricted to a period of five years only. Similarly, vide section 46-A, letting and sub-letting by the members, of scheduled castes and scheduled tribes had to be to the members of their respective communities only. For remedial action, Section 175 of RTA had to be gone through carefully. On any transfer and sub-letting in contravention of provisions of RTA, both the tenant and any persons who may have thus obtained or may thus be in possession of the land, or the part, were liable under section 175 of RTA to ejectment from the area so transferred or sub-let on an application of the land holder. Hence, vested interests spread the rumours that if at all they were rejected under the above-mentioned provisions, they would insist on the ejectment of the concerned tribal tenant also which, though correct, would have defeated the very purpose. In case, the land was allotted to somebody else, the concerned tribal tenant got no relief especially in case of transfers other than by way of sale where he at least had the theoretical possibility of getting that land in near or remote future, though not in a single case this appears to have materialised in the past. The alternative of applying section 91 of the Rajasthan Land Revenue Act (RLRA) 1956, providing for a person to be trespasser if he came into possession of any land without lawful authority, had also to be excluded as it covered only government lands. The possibility of getting the section amended in such a way that any transfer of tribal land to non-tribal in contravention of law could be treated as encroachment with liability of action under section 91 of RLRA against the transferee was also ruled out in view of possible time lapse.

The practical experience and on the spot study had brought out the following types of land alienations from the tribals to non-tribals:

(a) Transfer through registered sale deed followed by mutation and relevant changes in the record of rights.

(b) Transfer through unregistered sale deed with mutation and changes in the record of rights.

(c) Transfer through registered deed but not followed by changes in the record of rights.

(d) Transfer through unregistered deed and not followed by changes in the record of rights.

(e) Transfer through mortgage, sub-letting, etc.

In the first two categories of cases, the course open was either to proceed under section 175 of RTA or a *suo moto* revision by Board of Revenue under section 84 of Rajasthan Land Revenue Act or a reference under section 82 of RLRA by the Collector of the district to the Board of Revenue as after considerable discussions, amendment to the section 91 of RLRA for making all transfers of land from tribals to non-tribals actionable in a summary way was not found feasible at that stage. The cases of unregistered land alienation, where record of rights had not been changed, had posed the biggest problem numerically and otherwise because such transfers had been effected on a mass scale as a result of terror created by the outsiders, forcing Adivasis to hand over their lands to them for a pittance. And once the lands were thus transferred, there was no question of handing over the same again to the tribals even after the satisfaction of the terms of agreement, if any. Mostly these agreements were one way, where tribals even did not know the contents thereof, before putting their thumb impression or the like. Amendment to the section 43 (E) of the RTA in 1975, providing for imprisonment up to one year in cases of unlawful possession after the satisfaction of mortgage deed, proved a very timely one in the circumstances because a few instances of deferent action by the administration were enough to convince those who still required to be convinced regarding the advisability of returning such lands to the mortgagors.

## Confronting Recalcitrance

The collection of authenticated information where land alienation had taken place with or without necessary changes in the record of rights, though started on a war footing, naturally took some time and still more time was required for the completion of all legal formalities. However, in view of the rising expectations among the tribals, it was not at all possible to wait any longer, and meanwhile, it was, therefore, thought proper to start action on-the-spot in regard to cases where record of rights had not been modified. However, no sooner the work of restoring such lands back to tribals by administrative action commenced, it became clear that though agitated to get back the possession of their respective lands, tribals were not at all cooperative when it came to their facing the bullies for effectively retaining the possession of the lands restored to them.

The terror had to be overcome before any effective beginning could be made of the process of emancipation of the tribals. Persuasion was now ruled out in the circumstances and especially after prolonged discussions with officials and social workers, because accustomed as these bullies had been to these methods in the past, they just ridiculed the very idea of handing over of these lands back to the legitimate holders or releasing those in bondage and the like. The availability of various arms with them on a liberal scale on account of area being dacoity prone was another problem because in an area where the very sight of a bully was enough to make a tribal shiver, a bully with arms was more than enough to keep these tribals at a safe distance, irrespective of the consequences for them. Therefore, it became clear that unless some of these bullies were removed from the area or their arms taken away, it was not at all possible to make a beginning in an effective manner. On return to the headquarters and equipped with an assessment of the situation, I, therefore, took up the matter with the government; and everywhere there was sympathy towards these tribals and support for their emancipation. An order, therefore, was issued regarding suspension of all the arms licences in the area laying a specific time limit for surrender thereof to the respective police station. The fear of punishment under the Arms Act for the failure to comply with the orders was enough to make all concerned to adhere to the order. The more notorious ones among the bullies who had earlier been identified could not believe when they were arrested in a swoop for detention under MISA. One of these bullies was an ex-platoon Commander of Rajasthan Armed Constabulary, who in addition to grabbing the lands belonging to the tribals had grabbed huge chunks of government and forest lands on such a massive scale that from a particular point of the land only his lands would be visible and nothing else. These twin actions coupled with simultaneous action on the part of tribals to *suo moto* take back the possession of their respective lands, of course with full administrative support, were enough to make the others reconcile to the changed circumstances; and here lay the beginning of the end of an era of tribals' exploitation. To give added teeth to both the dedicated tehsildars in the area, powers were conferred upon them under section 107/151 of Criminal Procedure Code. Throughout the area, police parties were posted with the tehsildars with necessary instructions to take care of slightest resistance on the part of bullies and exploiters in an appropriate manner. Every village had to be visited by them for on the spot hearings and necessary follow-up action there itself. To strengthen the administration, a new senior post in the Rajasthan Administrative Service was created for this work only, with the designation of Additional District Magistrate and Project Officer, and an officer with dedication was posted against the same. I myself kept on visiting the area very frequently. All these arrangements ensured that no case of a tribal went by default on the part of administrative machinery. The release of bonded labourers posed a very big problem because of their not having any means of subsistence. The landlords and bullies had united with a view to crush the tribals in general and the released bonded labourers in particular and had decided not to offer them any employment, thus making them realise the foolhardiness of not only their action but that of administrative machinery as well. Hardly did they realise that soon it would be the landlords and not the tribals who will be begging the services of the latter for sowing and also for harvesting on mutually honourable terms.

## Upshot of Positive Programming

In spite of pressure tactics employed by the landlords, tribals did not agree to work at a rate below the minimum wages prescribed by law about which they had been made aware of by the administrative machinery and social workers. They were also educated in the process to work either on daily or at the most on monthly wage basis as per their will without any element of fear. Meanwhile, government had also sanctioned some amounts for public works such as roads, and it was enjoined upon all concerned to give priority in jobs and works to tribals. The case for some *ex gratia* payments to the released bonded labourers was also taken up with the state government which, later on, granted a subsistence allowance to each one of these labourers for three months at the rate of ₹ 100 per month. All tribal children with education were located together with the surprising revelation that not a single Saharia tribal ever found a government job. To remedy the injustice, all such tribals were, therefore, given jobs suiting their qualification. Those with some literacy were appointed as peons but those with adequate educational qualification were absorbed in various jobs with the result that within a very short time, 30 of these tribal candidates could be posted as patwaris, police constables, teachers and lower division clerks, inspectors, etc., preferably in the area itself to the extent possible, so that in due course they themselves could become a source of strength to the tribals and the shyness on the part of tribals to face government and public functionaries for necessary relief could be done away with. Not only the tribals but also a suitable number of scheduled caste candidates with necessary minimum qualifications were also absorbed in various government departments because alongwith the tribals they had also been subjected to exploitation by the influential interests. The low percentage of literacy among the tribals and scheduled castes in the area had been precisely because of the fact that those already educated never got any job, and once they saw their own children working as patwari and police constable and the like, they were convinced about their own strength and about various jobs awaiting those who took up education. The programme initiated on the above lines got adequate legal support in due course of time with new legislation covering various aspects for the upliftment of the weaker sections under the 20-Point Programme. With the coming into force of the Bonded Labour Act 1976, the vested interests lost all hopes especially when they saw those resisting the attempts of administration on this front being sent to jails. With the moratorium on recoveries, suits and executions in respect of debts of small and marginal farmers, village artisan and agricultural labourers, under the Rajasthan Scheduled Debtors (Moratorium on Debt) Act, 1976, and Rajasthan Scheduled Debtors (Liquidation of Debt) Act, 1976, complete discharge of the debt of marginal farmers, rural artisans and agricultural labourers having an income up to ₹ 2,400 per annum, an immense relief, was granted which brought a benefit to the maximum possible extent in the area. Further relief occurred to the weaker sections by amendment to the Moneylender Act providing for summary dismissal of suits if the concerned money-lender did not have a licence at the time of advancing the loan or did not render statement of account periodically.

## Concerted Follow-up

The release from exploitation had to be followed up with simultaneous efforts for resettlement of all these tribals on a long-term basis. Their deployment on public works and the like gave immediate relief only. The educated among them got the jobs as already mentioned. But what about those who had been completely landless and, therefore, could not be restored land for their livelihood? The intensive land allotment drive in the area resulted in the allotment of about 45,000 bighas of land to 4,400 tribals with simultaneous necessary entries made in the land records and possession given to the allottees to minimise hardships on them later. But allotment of land to the landless or restoration of the land itself was not enough, because agricultural operations required finances for necessary inputs. Hence, apart from revitalising the existing branches of financial institutions, new branches of Central Cooperative Bank and Land Mortgage Bank were opened and all possible assistance rendered to the tribals in their enrolment in the above agencies. For making available inputs such as seeds and fertilizers, the marketing society was strengthened. All these facilities, by and large, minimised hardships faced by the tribals for taking up the agricultural operations in the very first kharif season, and by the time I was transferred in the last week of July 1976, I not only had the satisfaction of seeing the green crops in the fields of some new allottees or to whom land was recently restored but also of the harvested crop and tasting the *chapati* made from the wheat thus harvested. The number of those released from bondage in this small area reached an impressive figure of about 3,100 which was more than half of the total bonded labourers thus released in the whole of the state of Rajasthan. By the time I left, I also had the satisfaction of knowing the work done on the basis of independent surveys made by the Department of Economics and Statistics, Rajasthan, which revealed that from 3 June 1975 to 31 March 1976 only, the possession of land was restored in case of 62.25 per cent of area belonging to 68.75 per cent of scheduled caste households while it was 68.91 per cent of area belonging to 79.49 per cent of scheduled tribe households. Out of the total restored area, maximum benefit accrued to households having no land left with them at the time of the commencement of the campaign.

Further, out of the total loan of ₹ 228 lakh at the commencement of the drive, burden had been reduced by about ₹ 75 lakh as a result of the action of government agencies and also through writing off the same by the moneylenders by way of negotiations with the debtors—as a sequel to demonstration activity of what was going around them. Out of the above relief, the share of scheduled castes, scheduled tribes and others was ₹ 8 lakh, ₹ 45 lakh and ₹ 22 lakh, respectively. More heartening was the revelation that during this period loans taken by the scheduled castes and scheduled tribes was ₹ 0.59 lakh (or 2.33 per cent of the total) and ₹ 2.85 lakh (or 13.89 per cent of the total), respectively, thus leaving a balance of ₹ 17.29 lakh for others out of the total estimated loan of ₹ 20.73 lakh.

The exercise of making the members of SC and ST honourable members of the community in the above 9 months had not, after all, proved futile especially when I know in my heart that real impact of the programme was much more by the time I left the district in July 1976 as compared to what the survey had revealed up to March 1976. Further, on the one hand, pressure on exploiters increased with the lapse of time not only because of governmental action, but also because of increasing involvement of the tribals themselves in throwing away the shackles of exploitation by way of bondage etc., while on the other hand, the administrative machinery was geared to plan for a major developmental thrust.

It was hoped that aboriginals will get a chance to develop, while preserving and conserving their own cultural foundations, for which, in a very humble way, a base had been laid down by a dedicated team of officials, notwithstanding almost insurmountable obstacles in the process, which ultimately resulted in the transfer of all of them, though of course, one by one. Yet the flame kindled by their missionary efforts will no doubt keep on burning in the form of freedom that these tribals will continue to enjoy.

# 17

# Down Memory Lane

## Sri Ganganagar (1976–1977)

I.C. Srivastava

Down memory lane, two events relating to my tenure as the Collector and District Magistrate, Sri Ganganagar stand out sharply in mind's eyes. In the first week of August 1976, when I took over charge of my office, 'Emergency' was still in force and full flow. Encroachments on roads in urban areas were easily removed on lands declared surplus under Urban Land Ceiling Law. Surplus lands still in possession of the original landowners and cultivators in rural area were resumed and taken over by SDOs who also allotted the same under Ceiling Law to landless persons on a large scale. Sri Ganganagar then had five IAS officers—two under training and three posted as SDO besides me. Shri G.N. Haldea, Shri B.L. Meharda and Shri Gurdev Singh had done extremely well in the allotment of ceiling land so as to earn state government's appreciation. But Emergency had no other facets to justify itself.

After our facing the fury of floods in August 1976, state government, at the behest of Shri Sanjay Gandhi the then most powerful Youth Congress leader (supposedly also the man behind promulgation of Emergency in the country), had decided to launch a massive family planning drive by holding large surgery campus to operate upon persons, willing or otherwise, for sterilisation. The district achieved a target of over 20,000 operations within a period of four months (September—December 1976) as against 3,000 cases in preceding five months, which earned us an appreciation letter from state government 'seeing is believing'. This old adage was exemplified by the hard work put in by the then CMHO, Shri N.K. Sharma, and his dedicated team of surgeons. On the concluding day of the massive camp at Hanumangarh where over 2,500 persons were operated upon and sterilised in a period of four days, I found, to my utter surprise, three doctors sleeping in their operation gowns after keeping awake for 2–3 nights at a stretch not only for operations but for post-operative after care as well. I was touched to the core of my heart and tears welled up in my eyes as I watched the dedicated doctors on duty who put in heart and soul in their work, even though it was a part of Emergency mandate.

This sight of surgeons sleeping in their gowns is coupled with another fleeting glimpse of the flashback of my memory—the material support extended by local people, including Halwais, tent owners and others who had set up stalls and counters to provide food and other essential supplies on the spot. The response of people once invoked was spontaneous, quick and timely in conformity to the needs. Sri Ganganagar people always responded to the call for mobilisation and support in government's efforts and programmes be it facing the fury of floods or collections under National Savings Scheme or holding of revenue campaigns for disposal of revenue and land-related cases.

But family planning campaign organised under instructions of the state government, which had overtones of pressure and state coercion, did result in forcible action in many districts—leading to some deaths especially of women from operations or otherwise. Later Justice Kan Singh Commission constituted by Janata Party Government in 1977 to look into Emergency excesses did enquire into such cases. I also received a notice seeking my explanation and reply over death of a woman caused after sterilisation operation. During enquiry, it was brought out that this death was caused by some other ailment and was not due to the aforesaid operation. This reply satisfied the Enquiry Commission and I was saved the ignominy of appearing before the Commission to justify the organisation of family planning camps on a large scale.

Emergency was turned into a political instrumentality for achieving political gains but no action was taken to set right the alleged excesses, by Janata Party Government which came to power after throwing out Congress Government under Smt. Indira Gandhi. However, the memorable and unforgettable family planning campaign yielded lessons for me and my collectorate colleagues. Devotion to duties and hard work too should be put within the framework of rules and regulations and one should never lose human touch and humanitarian outlook and approach while discharging one's duties. Such an approach had helped me overcome my hesitation in releasing the salary of all government officers and staff on the eve of Deepawali in 1976 in order to enable them to celebrate the festival of lights. But this was not done in other districts. This measure, therefore, came to be termed as one of the 'excesses' of Emergency as salary of those government servants who were unwilling to undergo the sterilisation operation was to be withheld in accordance with the decision taken by the Chief Minister himself in regional meetings of officers.

This decision not being part of any rules and discretion proved better than valour for me and my colleagues, thanks to the timely advice given by my personal staff to release the salary as aforesaid.

# 18

# Land for the Landless

## An Unfinished Story

Abhimanyu Singh

From 1978 to 1983, I worked as District Collector, first of Tonk and then of Alwar. Reminiscing over this eventful and challenging period, one case remains etched in my memory. This relates to the restoration of approximately 300 *bighas* of agricultural land to scheduled caste families of Chandpur village from the illegal and forcible possession of a powerful and influential brahmin.

One of the most important aspects of a Collector's job is the daily hearing and redressal of public grievances. When I took over as Collector of Tonk in May 1978, my three predecessors in office had shared a total tenure of only 18 months. As a result, the functioning of the collectorate had been adversely affected and the administration in the *mufassil* areas had lost much of its effectiveness. No wonder, a large number of cultivators from far-flung villages came to see the Collector personally to seek relief and help.

### A Genuine Grievance

During the course of these personal hearings, which sometimes extended till 7 o'clock in the evening, I noticed that a group of 4–5 persons met me frequently and never appeared to be satisfied with my assurances that I would examine their case and take appropriate action. After a while I decided that I could not make them hang around the collectorate any longer without their becoming a burden on my conscience. I called for the relevant file from the Revenue Section of the collectorate and examined it page to page with help of my Personal Assistant, Akbar Ali Khan, whose dedication to duty and concern for the public was touching.

On examining the file, we found that the cultivators who had been seeing me had a very genuine case and were seeking relief from the government and the collectorate for more than a decade. They belonged to a small and remote village of Kusai Tehsil situated about 70 km from the district headquarters. Only 39 families resided in this village out of which all except two belonged to the scheduled castes. All the families were entirely dependent on agriculture and allied activities for their livelihood. Only a handful of villagers had benefit of any formal education. In September 1962, an agricultural cooperative society of landless persons of the village was registered and allotted 297 *bighas* of land under the Rajasthan Land Revenue (Allotment of Land to Cooperative Societies) Rules, 1959. However, soon after this event one brahmin by the name of Daya Ram became a member of the cooperative society by fraud and deceit.

### The Effective Clout

It would be interesting to go into the personality of this man who came to play such a dominant role in the affairs of the village. He belonged to one of the two *savarna* families of the village, was formally educated and was the owner of 100 *bighas* of land in his own right. His brother-in-law who belonged to the other brahmin family of Chandpur also owned 30 *bighas* of land. Daya Ram owned a *pucca* house in the tehsil headquarters at Kusai and resided there with his family. From time to time, he moved to his ancestral house in Chandpur to supervise agricultural operations on his farm. He had the reputation of being a person with considerable political clout and influence irrespective of whether the state government was controlled by the Congress Party or the Janata Party. At first, he was a worker of the Swatantra Party and in 1978 he was a close associate of a ruling party MLA from that area. It was widely believed that he financed the MLA's election to the State Assembly in 1977. Local employees of the Revenue, Cooperative and Police Departments were said to be in his pay, and therefore they could not dare to take any action against him.

Daya Ram owned a tractor and used it to cultivate large tracts of agricultural land. He was in league with some antisocial elements of Kusai who were involved in the illicit liquor trade. Daya Ram openly carried weapons and the villagers of Chandpur were terrorised by him. With his political and financial powers, he harassed and exploited cultivators belonging to the backward sections of society by forcibly occupying their agricultural lands. When any villager took up the courage to offer any resistance, Daya Ram used his contacts in the police to harass him and even got false criminal cases registered against some villagers. In brief, he was the classic rural oppressor.

With this kind of personality, Daya Ram had taken complete control of the affairs of Chandpur Agricultural Cooperative Society, soon after his joining. By the late sixties, he had systematically inducted big land owners and his relatives from outside to the membership of the society. Even his son who was a student was made a member of the society. On some pretext or the other, he removed the landless scheduled caste members from the membership of the society. Where this was not possible, he allocated land to them at will in such a manner that the most non-productive stretches were given to them for cultivation. A vigilant Assistant Registrar of Cooperative Societies got wind of the going on in this society and, therefore, he removed Daya Ram from its membership in March 1965, but in January 1967 he became a member once again by forging the signatures of the chairman. After that there was no stopping for him. An enquiry held later revealed that he took personal possession of about 130 *bighas* out of the 297 *bighas* allotted to the society. The cultivators on the rest of the land either owed allegiance to him or gave most of their produce to him in acknowledgement of his superiority.

## The Unavailing Probes

In May 1969, the Assistant Registrar, Cooperative Societies, Tonk, made an enquiry into the functioning of Chandpur Agricultural Cooperative Society, detected numerous irregularities and brought it under liquidation. Daya Ram went in appeal against this order, and in December 1969, his appeal was accepted by the Registrar,

Cooperative Societies. The liquidation order was set aside and the case was remanded to Assistant Registrar, Cooperative Societies, Tonk, for further enquiry. Daya Ram managed to ensure that no further action was taken for another four years. In January 1973, the society was brought under liquidation once again. However, this time Daya Ram went in appeal directly to the Minister for Cooperation in the state government who, in fact, had absolutely no jurisdiction in the matter, and in December 1974, the minister set aside the liquidation order. All this while, Daya Ram continued to enjoy the usufruct of the land.

Two years later, the Deputy Registrar, Cooperative Societies, Ajmer, happened to visit Tonk on a tour and this case was brought to his notice by the dispossessed cultivators of Chandpur. He appointed tehsildar, Kusai, and Assistant Registrar, Cooperative Societies, as administrators of the society in May 1976. But lo and behold! The Deputy Secretary, Cooperatives, Government of Rajasthan, set aside all these orders in October 1977.

This was not all. The aggrieved scheduled caste cultivators had submitted petitions to the Chief Minister and to the Governor of the state. The latter had written to the Collector in May 1977 and asked for a detailed report on the matter. An important member of the Lok Sabha had written to the then Chief Minister to institute a judicial enquiry into the matter. With the Janata Party government in power in the centre as well as in the state since early 1977, the leader of the opposition in the Lok Sabha had also written to the Collector about this case in September 1977. The District Vigilance Committee, of which the Collector was the chairman, had also been seized with the matter since January 1977. Notably, the District Vigilance Committees had been constituted in every district to look into cases in which relief or redressal to the public had been inordinately delayed because of red tape, corruption or lack of administrative coordination. Normally, such a committee is an effective instrument in the hands of the Collector to resolve such cases, but in this specific case, except for some officers being deputed to make an on the spot enquiry, nothing concrete had been done to provide assistance to the harassed scheduled caste families of Chandpur.

These were the stark facts which stared me in the face after I had studied the file. The governments of the Congress Party and later of the Janata Party had been proclaiming that they were determined to tackle cases of atrocities on the weaker section with a heavy hand. The District Collectors and Superintendents of Police all over the state had been instructed to constitute special squads of revenue and police officers to go round the countryside and restore possession of land to members of weaker sections who had been forcibly dispossessed of their lands. But here was a case where a group of cultivators from Chandpur had petitioned every possible authority in the state but to no avail. What more could they do and where could they go from here? These thoughts disturbed me and made me determined to do my utmost to restore possession of the society's land to its rightful owners.

## Two-Pronged Strategy

It occurred to me that until then, administrative action had been confined to bringing the society under liquidation and appointing administrators. This begged the problem. Daya Ram was able to thwart the judicial process with impunity and maintain physical possession of the land without let or hindrance. Therefore, I decided that our strategy should be twofold: First to bring the society under liquidation and to see that the orders of the lower functionaries were not set aside by anyone from the state headquarters, and second, to get physical possession of the land from Daya Ram. Fortunately, the Assistant Registrar, Cooperative Societies at Tonk, was a dependable and reliable officer whom I could take into confidence on this issue. On being briefed about the facts of the case, he showed his willingness to help and on 20 June 1978 (within 1 month of my taking over charge as Collector, Tonk), he brought the society under liquidation once again. Alas, the Additional Registrar, Cooperative Societies, Rajasthan, granted an *ex-party* stay against this order without giving us an opportunity of being heard.

This was the fifth time since 1969 that liquidation orders of this society had been rendered ineffective because of Daya Ram's connections at the state capital. It was obvious that Daya Ram could not be taken for granted, and merely defending the case in the court was not enough to deter him. In these circumstances, I decided that I would have to violate the time-honoured convention of not approaching the presiding officer of a court in regard to cases pending in his court. I drove to Jaipur to see the Additional Registrar, Cooperative Societies, personally and explain the background of the case to him. Though he assured me that justice would be done, I found that for various reasons we could not rely on his assurances completely.

So I launched the second part of my strategy simultaneously. On my return to Tonk, I summoned the Government Advocate to seek his advice. He was a first-rate lawyer and a very cooperative person. He drew my attention to the provisions of Rule 5(4) of the Rajasthan Land Revenue (Allotment of Land to Cooperative Societies) Rules 1959, according to which the state government was empowered to resume the land allotted to cooperative societies on the ground that conditions of allotment had been violated. Making this the basis of my argument, I sent a detailed report giving the entire history of the case to the Revenue Commissioner-cum-Secretary of the state government.

A copy of the report was endorsed to the Secretary to the Chief Minister. On my next visit to Jaipur, I met both these officers personally and apprised them of the situation. I also requested them to put informal pressure on the Additional Registrar, Cooperative Societies, to vacate the *ex-party* stay order granted by him in favour of Daya Ram. Both these gentlemen were extremely helpful, and for the first time I felt hopeful that something positive would emerge.

## An Aggressive Follow-up

Back in Tonk, I asked my Personal Assistant to keep the file relating to this case in his personal custody. We also decided to review the progress of the case at least once a week. My report to the Revenue Secretary was followed by four demi-official letters in the space of 2 months, and a detailed demi-official letter to the Secretary to Chief Minister requesting him to intervene. These were interspersed with numerous trunk calls to the Revenue Secretary to remind him to expedite resumption of land in favour of the government.

On 24 October 1978, we got the morale-boosting news that the Additional Registrar, Cooperative Societies, had upheld the liquidation order dated 20 June 1978 and had rejected Daya Ram's appeal. This was a tremendous shot in the arm for us because for the first time in fifteen years, Daya Ram had lost in appeal. On the other hand, we received the not-so-good news that under pressure from the local MLA (Member of Legislative Assembly), the Revenue Minister had decided to hear the resumption case himself and not leave it to the Revenue Secretary as was customary. The local MLA made it a point to be present at all the hearings in the Revenue Minister's chamber. When I got this news, I briefed Sub-Divisional Officer, Tonk, and deputed him to attend each hearing in Jaipur. On the basis of the feedback given by him, we realised that the enquiry reports available on the file were incomplete in certain important respects. To strengthen our case, another detailed enquiry was conducted by SDO (Sub-Divisional Officer), Tonk, and much to our delight, the findings went very much against Daya Ram and in our favour.

As time went by and yet with no decision coming from the government, we became apprehensive. The Revenue Secretary told me that the minister was under pressure from the local MLA and was likely to delay a decision in the case indefinitely. Our plan was to try to see that Daya Ram was unable to sow the *Rabi* crop of 1978 on the disputed land. However, these plans were foiled by the Revenue Minister's procrastination. Consequently, Daya Ram was able to sow and then harvest the *Rabi* crop and as the time for sowing the *Kharif* crop drew nearer, we sensed that this was our last chance of dispossessing Daya Ram. Taking courage in both hands, I proceeded to Jaipur to confront the Revenue Minister. He confessed to me that our case was solid, but he was in two minds as he could not resist the pressure of his party MLA. I reminded him that the then ruling Janata Party was committed to support the weaker sections of society and that this was a golden opportunity to demonstrate this commitment. I hinted to him that the Chief Minister was aware of the facts of the case and a decision against the legitimate rights of the scheduled caste cultivators of Chandpur could embarrass him and the Chief Minister. I also told him that the vested personal interests of a party MLA should not be allowed to come in the way of a correct judicial decision in favour of the downtrodden. Being a lawyer by profession, he was convinced by my arguments. I briefed the Revenue Secretary and the Secretary to Chief Minister about my meeting with the Revenue Minister and requested them to persuade the Minister further. I returned to Tonk hopeful of a favourable decision.

The SDO, Tonk, Deputy Superintendent of Police, Tonk, and Tehsildar, Kusai, were called for an emergency meeting to make foolproof arrangements to take over possession of the disputed land from Daya Ram, in anticipation of government orders resuming it. A flying squad consisting of senior police and revenue officers was constituted and kept ready to move to the village. On 11 June 1979, the Revenue Minister issued a well-drafted analytical order pronouncing that the entire 297 *bighas* of land allotted to the society had been resumed by the state government. On hearing about the order on telephone from the Revenue Secretary, we moved with lightening speed and took physical possession of the land on 13 June 1979. The flying squad under the leadership of SDO, Tonk, camped in the village to ensure that Daya Ram and his associates did not make any attempt to re-enter the land. The Sarpanch was taken into confidence, and he sanctioned the mutation entering the entire disputed government land in the revenue records on 25 June 1979.

The next step was the issue of a notification by the SDO, Tonk, inviting applications of individuals for reallotment of the land. We felt that it would be in the cultivators' interest if individual allotments were made to them. We also realised that Daya Ram could still make a backdoor entry by getting false applications submitted for allotment of land. To prevent him from doing so, the SDO and tehsildar camped in the village for three continuous days to scrutinise each and every application received for allotment. Once we were assured that the applicants were genuine landless persons belonging to scheduled caste families of Chandpur village, we decided to go ahcad with the allotment programme.

## Victory for the Poor

On the day fixed for allotment, that is 13 July 1979, it was raining heavily. As a result, the SDO's departure for Chandpur was delayed by a few hours. As he was stepping into his jeep to leave for the village, Daya Ram and the local MLA handed him a stay order issued by the High Court of Rajasthan preventing us from allotting the land. When the SDO returned to Tonk to give me this news, I was extremely disappointed and cursed the rains. We had lost a golden opportunity to allot the land for sowing of the *Kharif* crop. But we had won a minor victory all the same because Daya Ram had also been prevented from sowing the crop.

Having gone so far and having worked so hard to get the land released from the clutches of Daya Ram, there was no going back. I realised that I could be transferred at short notice and made haste. A round-the-clock vigil was kept at Chandpur to keep Daya Ram at bay. Through the active assistance of the Revenue Secretary, we approached the High Court for withdrawal of the injunction. We argued that in the present condition, the land was lying fallow and that this was a national loss. Daya Ram had been dispossessed, the land had been entered in the government's name and therefore he had no right to cultivate it. If the High Court desired, temporary allotment of the disputed land could be made to scheduled caste landless families of Chandpur until the final disposal of the case. On 21 November 1979, the High Court permitted temporary allotment of the disputed land to landless families of Chandpur village but only for a period of one year. The allotment was promptly made by SDO, Tonk, to 38 scheduled caste families who were given possession of their allotted land on the spot. Finally, the 20-year old monopoly of Daya Ram had been effectively broken. We knew that once the scheduled caste persons had been given physical possession of the disputed land, it would be difficult to dispossess them after one year.

Until I left Tonk in December 1980, there was no interference in the peaceful cultivation of this land by the allottees. Today, I am not aware of the final High Court order or of the situation prevailing in Chandpur. Many a time, I have thought of enquiring about the welfare of my scheduled caste friends of Chandpur, but have refrained from doing so, believing that sometimes, no news is good news.

[Note: Names of most places and persons are assumed and not actual in this narration.]

# 19

# At a Point of Time

M.L. Mehta

The Sunday that fell on 19 July 1981 proved to be a day of crisis for the HCM, Rajasthan State Institute of Public Administration. Though it had been raining incessantly since 17 July, no one could have had any premonition of what was to come. The campus community woke up to a leisurely Sunday morning. The rising level of water on the western slope towards Jawaharlal Nehru Marg did not cause any anxiety till about 7.30 a.m. when the water level rose further and entered the houses occupied by K.N. Bhargava, the then Director of the Institute, and D.S. Kochar, Deputy Director. As a rare coincidence, Bhargava and Kochar and their wives were not in Jaipur. When the junior Kochars got marooned, they were rescued by the heroic efforts of the mess staff who risked their lives to rescue the children. The rescuers had to wade through waist-deep water to reach Kochar's house for providing help to the terror-stricken children. Around 8 a.m., Gopal, a waiter in the institute mess, came running towards the institute building and informed incredulous faculty members that the building had collapsed. None of them believed him. Eyewitness accounts of the tragedy revealed that it all happened within 10 minutes. Heavy rush of water caused by 33 inches rainfall in 72 hours and choking of two drain pipes led to overtopping of water at the Malviya Regional Engineering College crossing and the road breached. Consequent release of water led to sucking of sand from underneath the foundations by retrogression and the building just collapsed.

People were awestruck and bewildered by this enormity of the damage. Almost half of the building was washed away. All faculty rooms including the office of the Director, the establishment section, the record room, four classrooms and the reference room of the library were washed away. The most tragic and irreparable loss was the entire collection of research journals. Out of a total plinth area of 47,000 sq ft, about 22,000 sq ft was no more and what remained was unusable.

The damaged building had a ghastly appearance with a refrigerator and almirahs hanging from the first floor alongwith the grid-shaped concrete facade. With the sucking of sand from underneath, the foundations of the building not only came tumbling down but deep and wide ravines also got formed all around the damaged building, which looked like a battle-scarred fortress. The width of the ravines varied from 10 to 300 ft and depth from 50 to 70 ft. The shape of ravines inspired some people to suggest that this place should be used for training in anti-dacoity operations. Some thought it to be a good site for making swimming pools. These were bizarre responses to a great tragedy that had fallen on the institute.

The damaged institute became an instant tourist attraction. The city dwellers and casual visitors came in thousands only to be dumbstruck at the nature's fury. Ironically, it became a show place of Jaipur's flood destruction. People felt a sense of pity for the institute. None of them thought that it would rise again. However, it did rise again magnificently like a phoenix from its ashes.

### Earlier Growth

The formation of a nucleus, from which the institute grew, took place appropriately on Prime Minister Jawaharlal Nehru's birthday in 1957 as RAS *Training School* at Jodhpur. Two visionaries in M.L. Sukhadia, the then Chief Minister, and B.S. Mehta, the then Chief Secretary dreamt of creating a training centre of excellence. As the Officers' Training School went through various phases of growth, this vision was fulfilled. When Jodhpur proved to be an unsuitable location, for the institute, the OTS, as it was then known, was shifted to Jaipur (1963). The initial vision of creating a regional training facility for administrative cadres of the North Zone states led to selection of the present site of the institute, which spread over 70 acres and having a beautiful backdrop of a hill feature. The new campus was inaugurated on 15 October 1966, by Chief Minister M.L. Sukhadia. As expected, the Officers' Training School grew from strength to strength and soon blossomed into a reputed institute of learning. Its main phases of growth can briefly be enumerated as follows:

- *14 November 1957*: The institute was founded at Jodhpur as Officers' Training School for training of members of the newly constituted Rajasthan Administrative Service.
- *1959*: It took up the responsibility for professional training of IAS probationers of the Rajasthan cadre.
- *1961*: The Accountants Training School of the Government of Rajasthan was merged in it.
- *1963*: The institute was shifted from Jodhpur to Jaipur.
- *1966*: The present campus in Malviya Nagar, Jaipur, was built and occupied and Commercial Taxes School was merged in the institute.
- *1967*: The Ford Foundation began assisting the institute in strengthening library, teaching and research facilities and also in faculty development.
- *1969*: It was rechristened Harish Chandra Mathur State Institute of Public Administration to commemorate the memory of a distinguished administrator and parliamentarian from Rajasthan.
- *1979*: The institute began holding all-India training programmes sponsored by the Department of Personnel and other ministries of the central government. The Subordinate Accounts Training School was also merged in the institute.

The state government not only gave financial support but also provided quality and continuity in leadership in the institute. It is not insignificant that, during 25 years of its existence, the institute had 13 directors with an average stay of about two years. The faculty was also chosen with care. The superior quality of the staff created an atmosphere of hope, buoyancy and dedication, which, in turn, influenced trainees in their formative period.

The institute earned a national reputation. Most of the faculty members, including the Directors, were sent for study abroad. What they saw abroad broadened their vision, increased their commitment and strengthened their determination to develop the institute. The Department of Personnel, Government of India, also entrusted the institute with certain key training programmes in development administration.

## Aftermath of the Flood Havoc

This was the institute that was devastated on that fateful Sunday of 19 July 1981. A question mark loomed large about the very existence of the institute at Jaipur. The suddenness and severity of the blow added to the depth of the despair. There was no place for the faculty to sit in, no room for organising classes and no road to reach the institute. Whatever portion of the building remained was dangerously perched on a sandy island surrounded by deep and wide ravines and entangled in tonnes of enmeshed steel. Absence of K.N. Bhargava who had gone away to Delhi and was unable to reach Jaipur due to disruption of road, air and rail links for three days, made the task of rehabilitation even more difficult. The campus community worked as a team and undertook the dangerous task of salvaging whatever they could from the wreckage. They were able to salvage most of the equipment and furniture and about 25,000 books which were all shifted to the hostel. Since training was not possible immediately after the damage, the trainees were sent back to their departments. The vacant rooms in the hostel accommodated the faculty and the staff, while the mess housed the library. In the absence of any major activity, the initial period of about 1 month was used for stock taking and drawing up possible scenarios for the future. For three days, the campus community passed through hell without any water, power or milk supply. Gradually, essential services were restored. The disruption of the road link made the campus residents marooned. Rising transport costs and inconvenience in reaching the city added to their despair.

## Approaching the Rehabilitation Task

I was posted as Director of the institute on 13 August 1981 and had the first glimpse of the damage on 17 August, when I visited the institute for a reconnaissance survey. Despite being only 82 miles away from Ajmer and even after reading the newspaper accounts of the disaster, I never thought that the damage would be so severe. One had to see it to believe it. The task of rehabilitation appeared hopeless but urgent and had to be tackled without a single day's delay. Therefore, the informal tea session with the faculty on the 17 August was converted into a meeting, and all basic decisions about restoration were taken then and there with active support from K.N. Bhargava. Everyone agreed that, whatever the back room tragedy, the show must go on. Now, looking back, I think our decision to restart the training programmes forthwith without getting bogged down in the inadequacy of the physical facilities or the immediate crisis created the initial breakthrough.

Important tasks to be taken up were identified and a time schedule was worked out for their completion. Progress was reviewed almost every day to avoid slippages. I used to get progress reports at Ajmer either on phone or from faculty members visiting Ajmer for consultations. I took a fortnight to wind up at Ajmer where I was working as Member, Board of Revenue, and joined the institute on 27 August.

The visit of the Prime Minister and other VIPs on 28 August boosted our morale and gave us assurance of appropriate help. The Prime Minister had made an appreciative reference to the institute in the North Zone meeting held at Srinagar a few years ago and was distressed to see the damage.

The visits were over and the time came for taking stock of the total situation and devising a strategy for action. Both the staff and the faculty members were apprehensive about the future. In order to get everyone on the same grid, a staff meeting was held two days later on 30 August. This meeting clarified many issues and removed many doubts. The discussions led to the realisation that the worst was over, and that everyone should contribute his mite to restore normalcy in the quickest possible time. We did not want to get obsessed with the problem of restoration and, therefore, the tasks of systems improvement, exploring new areas of training and expansion of physical and academic facilities, were tackled simultaneously. The psychological break provided by the crisis at this point of time was used to revamp the systems and build afresh with innovative approaches. The tasks attempted fell into the following broad categories:

(a) Organising training programmes.
(b) Building up road link and restoration of civic amenities.
(c) Restoration of the damaged building and filling up of the deep gullies around.
(d) Construction of a new building.
(e) Expansion of training facilities.
(f) Creating new vistas in training programmes.
(g) Improvement of systems.
(h) Strengthening of recreational and games facilities.
(i) Environmental improvement.

### Training Programmes Recommence

As planned earlier, our first programme, after the flood havoc, began on 31 August 1981, for college Principals and Vice-Principals. Not having any classroom accommodation on the campus, we used premises available elsewhere. N.K. Kulshrestha did this course. Then we hired accommodation at the Institution of Engineers on Tonk Road and began a course for Junior Accountants there. Aparna Sahai bravely ran this outpost in September 1981. Gokul Bhai Bhatt graciously provided a conference hall under construction in the office building of the Rajasthan Khadi and Gramodyog Board on Jawaharlal Nehru Marg. M.K. Saxena of PWD gave admirable support and completed the work within a fortnight, and we were able to organise a seminar on Gandhiji on 2 October 1981. This technique of fixing up a date for a programme well in advance and then working backwards was utilised successfully by us many a time thereafter.

The logistics of running a programme on Tonk Road, about 8 km away from the institute via Jhalana Road, proved formidable. Non-availability of any suitable location nearby forced us to look inward. The innovative idea of erecting *shamianas* in front of the hostel solved most of our problems and by October, we were running five courses at a time under canvas. Even the prestigious Management Development Programme was done for the Government of India under canvas. The *shamianas* were obtained from the *farashkhana*. The thrill of running programmes under canvas was occasionally marred by the anxiety of an impending shower of rain or a dust storm. The trainees, the faculty and the staff shared the tribulations. When the rains came, the mess space or the small committee room was rearranged for the classes. Everyone prayed for the rains to stop. Rains often reduced the number of participants. In a course for MLAs, when P.C. Vishnoi, Speaker, Rajasthan Legislative Assembly, came for the inauguration, only one participant had arrived. Without betraying any anxiety, I first took him to see the damaged building, then showed him our construction plans and observing that even by then only three participants had come, invited him for a cup of tea. Only five MLAs had reached when we finished our tea and the course had to begin with five participants only. The Chief Guest, however, was very gracious in saying that the size of the audience made no difference to him.

Thus, by October 1981, we were back in the game with gusto. We felt emboldened to give an assurance to the LBS National Academy of Administration, Mussoorie, that a training programme for IAS officers from all states could be run in January 1982 in the institute premises. The promise was fulfilled.

### Building a Road Link and Restoration of Civic Amenities

The civic amenities were restored without much difficulty, but the construction of the road link proved a difficult task. A temporary path was built, up and down the *nullah* slope, by the campus community. Then, the campus officer, Hari Singh, took the initiative and imaginatively built what we then used to call, *Hari Singh Jhoola*. L.B. Baxi and his team helped us a great deal by agreeing to provide an approach road across the *nullah*. This link, involving heavy filling, was built in a record period of six weeks. Within a day, permission was obtained from the Forest Department to build a road through the forest land, and N.R. Mathur and his team, notably S.R. Bansal and Mahadeo, did the rest. On a suggestion, N.R. Mathur was given a State Award for his work. Bansal, a junior engineer, and Mahadeo, *Jamadar,* were honoured by us in a function presided over by the Minister, PWD.

The road was completed on 14 November 1981 as per schedule. This was a vital link for access to the main city. The completion of the road was of help to everyone living on or coming to the campus. In the next monsoon season, this road too got breached many times. However, it always got repaired in less than 24 hours due to energetic action on the part of the PWD staff. Finally, in April 1983, we got our regular road link to Jawaharlal Nehru Road after the filling of deep ravines.

### The Damaged Building Is Made Usable

Restoration work on the damaged building began in November 1981. Removal of the overhang was risky as it involved cutting of steel frames and beams from dangerous positions and pulling down heavy masses of concrete. The PWD once again did a splendid job.

Since only half the space was available, ingenuity was needed for accommodating the expanded faculty and staff without reducing classroom space. The seminar hall and library halls were partitioned to provide office and faculty accommodation and also to yield two classrooms. With this, we could run seven programmes at a time in the remaining building.

The ravines formed around the building were too dangerous to be left alone. Initially, we thought of building a girdle park there. On the suggestion of C.B. Mathur and Harbinder Singh, we decided to fill them up. In the first stage, NSS volunteers came forward and did the sandbagging during their annual camp held in the institute in December 1981. Filling up such a large area was no easy task. R.J. Majithia, the then Relief Commissioner, appreciated the situation and allowed us to go ahead in anticipation of the sanction and to complete it before the monsoon lest the building should get damaged again. It involved massive transportation of sand. About 100 tractors were pressed into service daily from April 1982 and the job took 6 months for completion. The sanction, however, got delayed for some reason or other and came only after ₹ 18 lakh had already been spent. Rajendra Jain and M.M. Singhvi helped a great deal. Two precious lives were lost in this operation, one by accident and the other by landslide. The main entry and the facade were redone with another grant of ₹ 8 lakh.

## A New Building Comes Up in Record Time

Even before the central assistance was received, we decided to get the foundation stone of the new building laid on the Foundation Day, falling on 14 November 1981. Our ideas about the new complex were firmed up and some plans were ready when a sanction of ₹ 100 lakh came in October. The work was entrusted to the Rajasthan State Bridges and Construction Corporation (RSBCC). Visits were made to the Management Development Institute, Gurgaon, and the Indian Institute of Management, Ahmedabad, to get ideas for the new building. Faculty members and staff worked out do's and don'ts about the building and had about 80 hours of interaction in all with V. Behal, Architect, on the design and functional layout.

Shiv Charan Mathur, Chief Minister, laid the foundation stone of the building on 14 November 1981. The dedicated team of RSBCC, led by J.M. Malhotra, M.C. Sharma, P.K. Lauria, Kamala Kant and A.P. Dalvi, completed the building, costing about ₹ 77 lakh in a record time of 18 months. Raj Mal Jain, Ram Rikhyani and Raj Purohit worked with commendable involvement.

It was a delight to see the structure coming up. Our active involvement in the project added to the pleasure. At every stage of construction, the architect, RSBCC, as builder and we as users, were in constant dialogue.

## New Organizational Structures Come Up

In order to create some degree of autonomy and flexibility in operations, we initially considered the possibility of converting the institute into a society. Due to many operational problems, this idea was given up and, instead, we formed, in November 1982, a Centre for Management Studies (CMS) as an autonomous society with financial support from state undertakings. This innovation in structure would allow us to reap the advantage of being a state institute and also an autonomous centre. The CMS is responsible for industrial management training and plays a complementary role to the institute. M.M.K. Wali, but for whose vision it would not have come up, was made the Chairman of the centre.

In March 1982, a Centre for Rural Development was created. Under a central scheme, an assistance of ₹ 13.75 lakh was received for this purpose. This led to creation of faculty positions in the disciplines of area planning, sociology, rural credit, agricultural economics and demography. A few rooms were also added in the hostel with this amount.

## Training Facilities Get Regionalised

In 1982, we held orientation training programmes for *Zila Pramukhs* and *Pradhans.* Impressed by our efforts, the Department of Rural Development handed over their State Institute of Community Development and Panchayati Raj, Udaipur, to us. This became possible due to the efforts of Anil Bordia, Development Commissioner and Sheesh Ram Ola, Panchayati Raj Minister. With a beautiful campus, it has become, on its reorganisation, the Udaipur campus of RIPA.

In order to reduce pressure on the institute at Jaipur, four regional centres, at Kota, Jodhpur, Bikaner and Udaipur, for training of junior accountants were sanctioned from 1 April 1983. These regional nuclei are bound to grow in the years to come.

## Training Moves to New Frontiers

The training programmes took on many new dimensions during this period. Some of these are as follows:

1. From 1 April 1982, the foundational course of training was made compulsory for all State Services at the entry point itself. This is unique in the country.
2. In order to familiarise trainees with the departmental working, an institutional phase extending up to 4 weeks was added after the foundational training.
3. For raising the capability of district administration, training programmes were run in the districts. The mountain had come to Mohammed!
4. Emphasis was laid on group work in training so that experiential learning took place.
5. Workshops and seminars were organised on alternative development strategies in various fields.

6. Courses have been planned in various functional areas within the departments.

## Systems Improvement

Various systems and procedures were revamped. A central facility by way of Teaching Material Development Cell was created. A training film library was set up. For considering long-term planning and development, a Policy Planning, Development and Coordination Committee was formed while the Programmes Committee was made more functional. A system of regular review of the programmes to be held and conducted was introduced.

## Games and Recreational Facilities Expand

Realising the importance of learning on play fields, a table tennis hall, two indoor badminton courts and two volleyball courts were constructed. It was intended to put up one basket ball court later on. Trainees are encouraged to play games regularly.

A recreation hall of 55′ × 35′ size was built over the new mess for the trainees to spend their evenings together. *Suruchi,* a film society, was registered for exhibition of films. The society would also arrange variety entertainment programmes. A big multipurpose hall, 80′ × 60′, has been built for screening of films.

## Greening of the Campus

A concerted programme was started in 1982 for greening the campus with the support of trainees, staff and faculty. So far, about 1,500 plants have been planted on the campus. For commemorative plantation, a *Smriti* society has been registered. The society takes ₹ 100 for upkeep of the plant from the person who wishes to plant a tree in memory of some personal event. K.K. Gupta, Bharat Singh, O.P. Mathur, V.S. Saxena, Captain Sood and A. Ghosh gave us good help in afforestation.

## In Retrospect

All in all, it has been a memorable experience battling through adverse conditions, seeing help coming when most needed, thinking and working day in and day out for converting the crisis into a boon and witnessing the staff performing their arduous tasks with dedication. The faculty also gave their best. Running larger number of courses, with half the building destroyed, demanded a high degree of adaptation, tolerance and commitment, and they showed it in plenty. Their efforts made the performance of this stupendous task look easy. Our high performance was also due partly to the high levels the institute had reached earlier as a result of the dedicated efforts of my predecessors and the ex-faculty members.

Help came from many quarters, expected and unexpected, and it would be difficult to name all these here. Both S.C. Mathur, Chief Minister, and M.M.K. Wali, Chief Secretary, gave great support and encouragement. They visited the institute very frequently, and this is an indication of the importance they attached to the institute.

I had the privilege of being the Director of the institute at a point of time of great historical opportunity of rebuilding after the crisis, which the US Ambassador, Barnes, himself a career officer, envied during his visit to the institute. The crisis generated a magnificent response from everyone in the institute, of which any organisation can just be proud. The significance of the response lies in the fact that it led to multidimensional growth in the institute. Long after, when the events are forgotten, those of us who were closely involved in the work fondly remember the effort and the teamwork that went into rebuilding the institute after the crisis.

Today, Rajasthan can justifiably be proud of rebuilding the best State Training Institute of Public Administration in the country. The flood havoc proved a blessing in disguise. As a result, we now have twice the space (1 lakh sq ft) we had before and also the organisation and systems to create excellence in the training field equal to the best anywhere in the country.

# 20

# Panchayati Raj

## By the People, for the People and of the People: A Case Study

**Rajendra Bhanawat**

Shahpura is a Panchayat Samiti of Bhilwara district in Rajasthan. District Bhilwara has made progress at a fast pace during the past few years. Besides Shahpura, there are 10 more Panchayat Samities in this district. The Pradhan of this Panchayat Samiti was known for terrifying people in that area. Only those officers, who fell in line with him, could continue in Shahpura. A BDO who had the courage to challenge his authority was beaten up. The office of Panchayat Samiti was apparently run by the Pradhan, and no paper could move in and out of the office without his explicit consent. There were a number of criminal cases pending against him for some of his nefarious activities. The matter went up to the Supreme Court, which asked the Collector of the district to give a detailed enquiry report. The Pradhan had been suspended during the pendency of this enquiry. With the installation of the new Chief Minister, he not only got himself reinstated, but also saw to it that all cases against him were withdrawn. So, his criminality got a boost, and he started behaving in a more authoritarian manner. This man claimed that he was very close to the Chief Minister.

It was at the same time that the government thought of reviving the almost defunct Panchayati Raj keeping with a clutch of decisions and follow-up instructions. One of the measures towards strengthening the Panchayati Raj Institutions in the state was to create the posts of Chief Executive Officer (CEO) in each district to be held by either an IAS officer or a Selection Scale State RAS officer. I was posted as CEO in District Bhilwara, the home district of Chief Minister.

According to standing orders of government, the teachers in the primary schools were appointed by Panchayat Samities, but then selection was made by the District Establishment Committee (DEC) headed by Zila Pramukh, Collector being its member and CEO (then ADDO) its Secretary. Until such time, regularly selected teachers were made available by the DEC, the Panchayat Samiti had the powers to appoint ad-hoc teachers whose services were to be terminated as soon as the selected teachers were available.

In accordance with the general decision taken in the state, DEC made selection of about 1,000 teachers who were allotted to different Panchayat Samities, depending on their preference and their merit position. Most of the teachers selected were already working as ad-hoc ones but there were quite a few who were to replace the ad-hoc teachers. This would mean termination of services of ad-hoc teachers.

While almost all the Panchayat Samities followed the guidelines of the state government and Zila Parishad and gave appointment to DEC selected teachers, despite my pursuance, Pradhan Shahpura refused to give appointment to 40 teachers or so who were to replace ad-hoc teachers appointed by him. He, however, gave appointment to 27 others, who were already working in his Panchayat Samiti on ad-hoc basis. The Pradhan did not bother for letters and telegrams sent by the CEO to comply with government's instructions to give appointment to the DEC selected teachers. It is relevant to mention here that the DEC had made selections before the new CEO joined.

The BDO, the official Head of PS, was unable to comply with the instructions of Zila Parishad due to the threat and pressure of the Pradhan. The BDO, basically a teacher, was working in an officiating capacity. He was a spineless fellow and could not dare to act against the wishes of the Pradhan. When the CEO saw no way out to appoint newly selected teachers, he decided to call the BDO and ask him to issue appointment orders from district headquarters. It became necessary because the orders had to be issued under the signatures of the BDO. As the powers of CEO had not been defined under various Panchayat acts and rules, he thought it appropriate to apprise the Collector of the situation and take him into confidence. The Collector, after listening to the whole episode, advised the CEO to wait till he had talked to the Chief Minister as the action suggested was very drastic and could have wider repercussions. The CEO, however, had the view that the matter of giving appointment to selected teachers was of routine nature, so there was no need at all to consult the CM. In any case, he agreed to postpone the decision of calling the BDO for a day or two, till the Collector talked to the CM. He did so next day, and the message conveyed was that the CM wanted the things to be done in a judicious manner according to rules.

As the CEO was not sure that the BDO would come of his own accord, he asked the Tehsildar to send the BDO with someone on a motorcycle. The BDO was called in the Circuit House, where the CEO was staying. Concerned officers of Zila Parishad, along with relevant records, were also there. The BDO was asked to make a list of postings of newly selected teachers. He was given a free hand in deciding about the places to which the new teachers were to be posted. By evening, the cyclostyled appointment orders were posted to all newly selected teachers and the services of all ad-hoc teachers were terminated from the day the new ones joined.

For the next 10–12 days, the teachers kept on making the complaint that the ad-hoc teachers were not handing over the charge to the newly appointed teachers because of the instigation and protection of the Pradhan. They also informed that the Pradhan had put his muscle men in villages to prevent the entry of newly appointed teachers. The CEO assured the teachers that they could assume charge and inform through postcard. Besides full police protection would be provided, if needed.

After about a fortnight of issue of the orders by BDO, i.e., appointing of new teachers, some teachers came to CEO and produced before him a copy of the order of BDO withdrawing the earlier order and putting the ad-hoc teachers back into job in place of the new appointees.

The CEO immediately talked to Collector and drew out a plan of action. On his report, the suspension order of the BDO was issued by the Collector, as the BDO had reversed his own orders within 15 days under pressure of the Pradhan. Besides, the Tehsildar was asked to take over the charge of BDO and come to district headquarters immediately. As soon as the Tehsildar arrived at the headquarters, an order was signed by him cancelling the order of BDO withdrawing the appointments of ad-hoc teachers. This order of Tehsildar, in capacity of BDO, meant that the ad-hoc teachers were again out of job, and the new ones were to continue. It was also made clear that salaries would be paid only to those who were appointed on the basis of DEC selection. About 27 of these 40 teachers joined and were posted in remotest possible areas. It was also rumoured that the Pradhan's keenness in retaining the ad-hoc teachers was due to the fact that he had taken more than ₹ 4,000 for each appointment and terminating them would create problem for him.

Hurt by this unexpected turn of events, the Pradhan rushed to Zila Parishad and managed to get a meeting of the Collector, Zila Pramukh and Pradhan fixed. Strangely enough, in the absence of the CEO, a decision was taken in this meeting to retain the new teachers as well as the old ones. This meant that 27 teachers would be working over and above the sanctioned strength of the Panchayat Samiti. This was done in anticipation of getting 20 new posts for 10 new schools. It was not clear as to how the ad-hoc ones would be paid salary till the sanction was issued. The CEO, on his return from tour, came to know about such an arbitrary decision and apprised the Collector of his apprehensions. But nobody seemed to be bothered. Though the Zila Pramukh was not very happy with the Pradhan, even so he agreed to a decision, which was administratively and financially irregular. Other Panchayat Samiti Pradhans also started raising their voice for taking back in service the already terminated ad-hoc teachers. Soon after, I got my transfer orders from District Bhilwara.

# 21

# Family Planning Camp

## An Incident

**Sudhindra Gemawat**

Only the other day, I was passing through a street in Jaipur when two scavenger ladies were talking. I overheard their conversation. One was telling other, 'After all your husband is not a Collector'. This shows the importance of this post in the minds of the people even today.

In the year 1985–1986, I was posted as Collector and District Magistrate, Sikar. During this period, one event that I still remember relates to a Family Planning Camp at village Ajeetgarh in Neem ka Thana—subdivision. That day, I was sitting in my office at Sikar when a wireless message was received in the afternoon at about 2 p.m. from the camp in charge. It said, 'Matter serious, come immediately'. I was surprised to see this message because the sender was the camp incharge and not the police nor the revenue administration. I rang up the police station at Neem ka Thana, and I was informed that SDM and Deputy SP had gone to the Family Planning Camp. Station reported that everything was normal and no serious incident had occurred. I then got in touch with Superintendent of Police Shri R.S. Dhillon. He also did not report anything serious but I had my own doubts. I told him that there was something wrong somewhere, and we should visit the camp. If there was nothing, we would have a round and come back. He agreed to my suggestion, and we left Sikar at 3 p.m. and reached the village at 4 p.m. We first went to the police station and enquired about the incharge. We were told that he had gone to the Family Planning Camp and the situation in the town was normal. We reached the camp site, which was in the local dispensary premises. There was lot of rush, and people were preparing to leave. They were being given the incentive amount and some utensils by local donors. Doctors were still busy with the operations, whereas social workers were attending the operated patients and their relatives. The whole atmosphere looked like a fair. We were happy that nothing untoward had happened, and the wireless message was somebody's prank. We then entered the dispensary and met the Camp incharge Dr (Smt.) Kabra, who was a Senior Surgeon at Government Hospital at Sikar. She took us to the local doctor's residence, which was within the premises of the dispensary, and informed us that a lady had come from a nearby village for the family planning operation. To prepare her, they gave her an injection and within 10 minutes she was dead. Probably the injection had reacted. All other patients were also given the same injection but nothing happened to them. She did not know what had gone wrong.

I enquired of her, if the fact of the lady's death was known to her family members and others in the camp. Dr Kabra informed us that this fact was not known to anybody except the operating doctors. I asked! 'What about her family members?' Her answer was, 'No, they are anxious and are repeatedly asking us as to why she is not being sent out if she has been operated. We have informed them that she is not well and we are looking after her. Though this has not satisfied but we had no option'.

Then we told her our plan.

I told her that we could not declare her death then and there. This will create law and order problem. Such incidents had taken place elsewhere in Rajasthan where people had become unruly and had started raising slogans and pelting stones. Doctors and the staff had to run for their lives and had to hide themselves from the public fury. 'So the best course is to keep the body inside the dispensary. Tell the relatives that the lady has developed some serious complications and she is to be taken either to Sikar or to Jaipur for which we are making arrangement'. I also asked her to prepare a vehicle in which the patient was to be kept on a stretcher, put oxygen mask and a drip on her and also asked her to send a doctor and nursing staff to accompany the patient to Sikar and tell her relatives to go with the patient in the same vehicle. 'Wait till the crowd melts and leave the village only when it gets a little darker. We will be sitting at the police station, which is outside the town on the road side. If there is any problem earlier, inform us immediately', I added.

At about 6.30 p.m., the truck carrying the patient passed by the police station in our presence. In the meanwhile, we instructed Chief Medical Officer, Sikar, of the incident and asked him to be ready to receive the patient and start treatment on her arrival. Within one hour, the body of the patient reached Sikar Government Hospital where apparently treatment was continued.

At about 10 p.m. CMHO informed me that the patient had been declared dead and her family members informed. I told him to arrange for the return of the dead body to her village. We also informed the concerned police personnel to accompany the dead body to the village and to see that funeral takes place tomorrow early morning.

A sum of ₹ 10,000 was also sent to the family of the bereaved, which was as per rules.

On the day of the event, late in the evening a telephone call was received from the local MLA to enquire about the case. I had to tell him that the patient was in hospital receiving treatment. Probably, he might have sensed that there was something abnormal.

Anyway, the whole episode was handled carefully, and we avoided a confrontation and a probable law and order situation. The family of the deceased never raised any protest but I felt sorry for the seven kids who had lost their beloved mother.

# 22

# Changing Face of Administration

**B.D. Joshi**

Gradually, administration has become more difficult and complicated affair. With ever-rising corruption, political interference and deteriorating law and order situation, administrator has to remain more alert, vigilant and keep huge patience.

Things were not so difficult twenty years back when I and many of our colleagues were working in the state administration and had to face many difficult situations. No doubt corruption was there in those days also, but it was not so rampant and there was a sense of fear in subordinate staff. Number of scams were also few, and by and large there was respect for law and regard for honest and bold officers. Politicians also used to give more weight to the opinions and advice of officers. Transfers were rare and most of them were either on merit or need-based. I had an opportunity to serve as the District Magistrate in four districts namely Dholpur, Sawai Madhopur, Sikar and Ajmer. To illustrate what has been mentioned above, it is worthwhile to narrate a few instances that happened during my tenure in few of these districts.

I recall an incident that happened during my tenure as the Collector and District Magistrate, Sawai Madhopur in the year 1987. Only due to speedy action and prompt decisions and whole-hearted cooperation of political parties and fellow officers that it was possible to control one of the most difficult communal problems occurred in Gangapur town. It was on account of clash between two groups of students in Government College, Gangapur. In this clash, a student belonging to Mohammedan community stabbed another who was Meena by caste and he died on the spot. Two other Meena students were also seriously injured and had to be taken to local government hospital. This enraged other students also and hundreds of persons including students took out a huge procession and assembled before Sub-Divisional Magistrate's residence shouting slogans.

It was by chance that on this particular day, I had come to Gangapur on my way to Nadoti village to attend Panchayat Samiti meeting and went to SDM's residence. Looking to the troubled situation, I immediately cancelled my programme and tried to pacify the mob, which was very aggressive and becoming violent. My assurance that immediately a party will be sent to apprehend the accused had some sobering effect. I also asked them to help us in sending the injured students to Government Hospital, Karauli, as there were no proper facilities available in local hospital. An ambulance was immediately arranged and injured persons along with the doctor and nurse were sent to Karauli. This had also pacified the mob to some extent. Unfortunately the mob had already taken charge of the dead body, and it was a big factor to aggravate the situation. There was no way out to disperse the mob as there were hardly 10 police personnel available at Kotwali, and SHO was also on leave. While arranging ambulance, I had an opportunity to contact Director General Police, Jaipur, DIG, Bharatpur, and Superintendent of Police, Sawai Madhopur. I explained to them about the grave situation and requested them to arrange as much police force as possible and send them expeditiously.

Since arrival of police force had to take some time, we had to engage the mob one way or the other. Due to prompt arrangement of sending the injured persons to Karauli and despatching a police party to arrest the accused person, they had established some faith and their aggressiveness had calmed down to some extent.

Meanwhile, a passenger train coming from Delhi had stopped at nearby railway station and it diverted the attention of most of the persons in the mob and they proceeded to railway platform with some sinister motives. In between, they also damaged one bus standing near railway station. At railway platform, GRP also tried hard to control them, and they could not do much harm on railway platform.

Luckily by the time, mob was returning back, sufficient number of police personnel had arrived from Bharatpur with DIG in command, and it could be possible to control the situation to some extent. With arrival of some more police force from Sawai Madhopur and Jaipur, it could be possible to promulgate Section 144 Cr. PC, which prohibited assembly of persons more than five and carrying arms. We also requested the shopkeepers to close their shops to avoid any damage by miscreants.

Though it was expected that the situation would normalise soon, but some of the Meena leaders tried to give this incident communal colour and one of their top leaders gave a call to his community members of nearby villages to assemble at Gangapur. By next morning, more than 500 persons had gathered in the town with dead body in their control. They had put many unrealistic demands before the administration, which could not be met. Prolonged negotiations were on, and we assured that adequate compensation would be given to the family and all necessary steps have been taken to arrest the accused person. Though most of the persons appeared to be satisfied with the action taken by the administration, but some of the leaders were very adamant and instigating others for violent actions. In view of this, few prominent leaders had to be arrested and one of them was sent to Sewar Jail at Bharatpur. We also advised the family members of the deceased student to take the dead body in their charge. After handing over the dead body, a quick funeral was arranged in the village to which deceased student belonged. With arrest of their leaders, most of the persons who had come from nearby villages went back. However, to ensure that this type of assembly may not take place again, some check posts were established outside the town with the instructions that no person with arms be allowed to enter the town. Though peace was restored in Gangapur town, but matter did not end there. Some Meena leaders did not leave their efforts to disturb the communal peace and large number of persons assembled at village sop, which was about 10 km away from Gangapur. Their number was about 2,000 as per intelligence reports. They did not hide their intention to attack the village Udai, to which the accused person belonged. They had also collected arms and few canons, which were lying idle at some of the places.

After assessing this grave situation in consultation with Superintendent of Police, Sawai Madhopur, DIG, Bharatpur, and Shri R.K. Baijal, IGP Headquarters, we came to the conclusion that local police and RAC personnel may not be able to face this type of situation. I requested Shri V.B.L. Mathur, the then Chief Secretary Rajasthan, that assistance of PAC would be necessary to meet this threat. He was kind enough to arrange this expeditiously. PAC was posted at strategic points to meet this situation. Meanwhile, we also formed a peace committee comprising representatives of all political parties in the area and few reputed members of the town and adjoining area, which also included some Meena leaders. We requested the peace committee members to go and meet the persons gathered at village sop and ask them to give up their plan to attack the village as it would result in grave law and order situation and may result in huge loss of property and persons. Meanwhile accused person was also arrested, and there was no reason to take this extreme step. News of the arrest of the accused person and arrangements made by the administration to meet the threat had also reached them. Efforts of peace committee were also very helpful to ease the situation. Wisdom prevailed on them, and they peacefully dispersed. This brought peace in the area, which remained disturbed for more than a week. State administration had all the praise for local administration, which brought normalcy without any loss to human life or property.

I had to face one more difficult situation, though of different nature and in another district, Sikar. It was first week of October 1987, when I had gone to Barmer (Rajasthan) on leave due to sad demise of my elder brother. At that time, I was Collector, Sawai Madhopur. I got an urgent message from the Chief Secretary, Rajasthan, in which I was directed to immediately proceed to Sikar where law and order situation had taken an ugly turn due to self-immolation by Smt. Roop Kanwar at Divrala on demise of her husband Mal Singh. It was being celebrated as glorification of Sati and thousands of people were visiting Divrala for Pooja and glorification, which was declared illegal by the state government. There was much resistance from certain self-appointed youth leaders, causing grave law and order situation. Daily demonstrations were taking place and district officials were finding it very difficult to face the situation.

I immediately proceeded to Sikar in a car provided by the Collector, Barmer, and reached by midnight 4 October 1987. Large number of persons had gathered at Sikar, waiting for the arrival of the new Collector, with number of grievances and problems remaining unsolved. There was acute famine in the district causing various problems such as drinking water, scarcity of fodder for cattle and providing employment to the labourers, as no famine works had started. On the other side, situation at Divrala and adjoining area was going out of control due to arrival of large number of persons for glorification of Sati in total defiance of law.

I have narrated this situation to show how I got cooperation from both politicians and subordinate staff to handle this problem. In the next morning, I arranged a meeting of all political parties and district officials and explained them prevailing situation and problems and my plan of action to solve them. They wholeheartedly approved my line of action and assured that no agitation would take place and they would fully cooperate with the district administration. It took a fortnight to control the situation at Divrala, for which some stern measures were taken but I got full cooperation from the residents of Divrala and adjoining area. They helped me wholeheartedly to normalise the situation. They did not allow any miscreants to disturb the peace in that area. They themselves took the lead in preventing the persons who were coming for glorification and thwarted their all attempts to disturb the area. We formed local committees to keep a strict watch about the situation and inform the Control Room, which was established in the Government Higher Secondary School. We also established police outposts at the places from which one could enter Divrala and nobody with arms was allowed to enter. A prohibitory order under Sec. 144 Cr. PC was already in force in Divrala, and no procession was allowed or speeches for glorification of Sati were permitted. Publicity material was also distributed in nearby villages and also in Divrala, which explained the legal provisions under which action could be taken in case of glorification of Sati. This helped us in bringing normalcy in the area, and it was a big relief to all of us who also had to meet the situation due to acute famine and provide quick relief.

In between, there was a visit of the Speaker of Lok Sabha, Shri Balram Jakhad, and he was very helpful in solving problems relating to famine. He arranged free fodder for cattles from Punjab. At that time Mr Ramdev Singh was the Minister for Cooperatives, belonging to Sikar and to my surprise he took keen interest in famine works and used to sit for long hours while sanctioning famine works. There was no complaint of any corruption from any quarter. There was no agitation nor grievances. This shows that if there is sincerity in approach, it would not be difficult to solve the problems.

Another instance relates to a clash between two communities at Pisangan in Ajmer district. Just after Holi celebrations, certain miscreants threw Gulal (red powder) on the members of another community, which was resisted. A wooden hut belonging to a poor fellow was also burnt. As soon as the report reached to me, I along with Deputy General Police and Superintendent of Police reached there and took stock of situation. Prohibitory orders under Sec. 144 of Criminal Procedure Code were imposed and those who defied it were arrested. Arrested persons belonged to both the communities. This brought peace in the town but minister belonging to the area was quite furious as certain miscreants were related to him. He wanted to visit the area, but it could have created more problems in the town, which was reaching towards normalcy. I had a talk with the then Chief Minister, and he was kind enough to intervene and minister's visit was postponed. Peace was soon restored and life became normal there. Local politicians and residents were very cooperative and brought harmony between both communities.

These instances show that cooperation was always forthcoming, if the efforts are sincere on the part of both officials and politicians. A vigilant eye could also curb the corruption. Decision should be quick and any laxity may prove very costly.

Situations have changed considerably. Cooperation between politicians and bureaucrats is less visible and sometimes they proceed in different directions. Decisions are delayed, which give rise to corruption and resentment among common men. Unsocial elements take full advantage of deteriorating atmosphere and crimes go on rising. A strong leadership is required to bring a positive change. Though certain measures have been taken to curb corruption, which includes enactment of Right of Information Act and providing citizen's charter, but it requires proper implementation. Transparency and accountability are two tools that can change mindset and inspire confidence in common people. Various recommendations have been made by the Administrative Reforms Commission but unless they are implemented, no positive change is possible in administration.

# 23

# Jaipur Riots of 1990

I.C. Srivastava

During July 1989—July 1991, I was posted as Divisional Commissioner, Jaipur. In the year 1990, in the wake of L.K. Advani's Rath Yatra to mobilise support for construction of Ram Temple at Ayodhya on the site of Babri Masjid, communal riots broke out in several parts of the country. Jaipur, the capital city of Rajasthan, had already experienced, in 1989, a communal riot, although on a low scale, in Shastri Nagar area of the city. The Ram Shilas were the bricks meant to be sent to Ayodhya for construction of Ram Temple with the objective to replace Babri Masjid. Ram Shila Pujan Abhiyan consisted of series of ritualistic functions organised in various parts especially in communally sensitive areas in the midst of Ram Shila Pujan campaign. The situation was brought under control with a swift and concerted action by the district administration. However, the smouldering fire ignited by the campaign to mobilise support for construction of Ram Temple led to the outbreak of communal riots in Ram Ganj area of the city, which was highly sensitive being densely populated with people of Hindu and Muslim communities living together in harmony over 200 years. The country's partition in 1947 had changed the outlook and lifestyle of people which has been slowly veering towards communal divide leading to mutual distrust and suspicion.

Political games based on vote bank politics have exacerbated the situation over the years.

A slight skirmish over the call for Jaipur Bandh and its enforcement by communalists led to the outbreak of riots on a large scale. When the situation went out of control, the then District Magistrate, Shri V.S. Singh, SP, Shri H.N. Meena and Shri A.S. Gill, DIG Jaipur Range, rushed to the area. As the news of riots spread to the other areas, people came out on the streets gathering in groups to muster support in case riot spread to their areas. Intelligence officials' feedback to state government sent alarm signals through the corridors of power.

The then Home Secretary, Rajasthan, Shri L.N. Gupta, a model civil servant in many ways, rang me up to say that intelligence and other reports being received by him indicated that situation in Jaipur town would go completely out of control if assistance from local army command was not made available immediately. A flag march by army troops and their strategic positioning alone would save the situation. I was already aware of the sensitivity and building up of the tension which could erupt into riots in many parts of the town any moment. In fact, the preparedness for this purpose of communalists had already been mentioned in the intelligence reports of the central and state police agencies. Shri L.N. Gupta, therefore, suggested that I should follow-up with army officers, his request to despatch army platoons and companies already made on phone a few minutes earlier. He also added that as Divisional Commissioner and also being a supervising officer over Districts Magistrate, if I could speak to the Brigadier in Command of Jaipur Cantonment that District Magistrate on return to his office from the field action would give the requisition for despatch of army units in writing would expedite action on the part of army officers. I lost no time and complied with his instructions by speaking to Brigadier and other army officers at length about the situation in Ram Ganj and other areas in precise terms so that they could easily and quickly grasp the gravity of the overall situation and also realise their moral and legal duty to come forward to assist Civil Administration. It was gratifying that army platoons rolled out of the cantonments in less than half an hour and reports were received after an hour from Chandpole and Tripolia

Bazar areas that flag march by the army had helped ease the tense situation by afternoon. When Shri V.S. Singh, D.M. returned to his office, he did send the requisition to army authorities required by law. It was accomplished as expeditiously as possible. Thus, our prompt action satisfied the army officers also.

Consequently, we were able to control and localise the riots in Ram Ganj area. Although a curfew which was clamped, remained in force for a week or so, town life was not completely paralysed as relaxation of two hours initially leading to completely lifting of curfew after a week did provide great relief for necessary supplies to be made through market as well as through mobile fair price shops. How curfew was properly enforced was seen to be believed. IG level officers were sitting at the police stations guiding as well as freeing the field officers to enforce curfew and carry out searches leading to recovery of large cache of arms and ammunitions.

The control and restriction of communal riots in Jaipur city in the year 1990 will not remain a forgotten story as police officers of the state as well as the magistrates came to learn their lessons in time, which certainly stood them in good stead because no major riots took place in Rajasthan in the wake of Mumbai riots of 1993 or other riots, which took place in other parts of the country.

However, a flag march by the army units on a verbal request of the Home Secretary, Rajasthan, and Divisional Commissioner will ever remain fresh in memory as a unique concerted action, which shows the resilience and steely strength of the state administration acting in unison with army.

# 24

# Election Impasse

## Churu District

Jagat Pal Singh

The incident relates to the State Assembly Elections—October 1993. Elections having taken place, the stage was set for counting of votes. As is the procedure, all the contesting candidates nominate their respective counting agents to watch their interest during the course of counting of votes.

After making necessary verifications, the District Election Officer authorises such agents to remain present at the counting (of votes) venue; they can raise objections if they see any violation of the counting procedure.

I had issued the agents passes, as per procedure, and the counting stage was ready. The counting was to begin at 2 p.m., the next day. After having made last minute preparations, I returned to my residence and retired after the day's work.

Divisional Commissioner, Bikaner, rang me at midnight. I was asked to withdraw the passes of counting agents who were for the regional political parties, to considerably reduce the number of the counting agents. The reason given for such a step was that in Bikaner district, there had been clashes between two communities and as such the presence of counting agents in the arena of counting might have serious repercussions and as such (the Commissioner informed me) the Bikaner District Collector had already withdrawn all the passes issued to the counting agents of candidates belonging to regional political parties. The Commissioner told me that as it was apprehended that similar law and order problem might arise in neighbouring districts, all the DEOs were being accordingly advised to withdraw counting agent passes. I was emphatically asked to take similar action in my district also.

I pleaded that the elections in my district had been absolutely trouble free and also that I had no apprehension of any law and order problem in Churu district. Cancellation of passes was bound to create complications, I submitted. I also brought to the notice of the Commissioner that the written instructions from the Election Commission, the State Chief Election Officer and also from the Commissioner's Office were in all matters, pertaining to election, the regional and national political parties were to be treated at par. I was in no position, therefore, to ignore such instructions. I also added that on record there was no fresh material to enable me to revise my earlier orders regarding the passes, which had been issued with the consent of the SP who had made some preliminary enquiries about the antecedents of the counting agents. I made it clear that any unwarranted cancellation of passes might agitate the contesting candidates and the election process was likely to be boycotted, and this might cause serious problems; my revised order could be legally challenged and I might be held responsible for this. I also pointed out that time at our disposal was too short for any mending of the situation and told the Commissioner that I could not cancel the passes.

After hearing me, the Commissioner told me in stern voice that if I did not act as advised, I would be responsible if anything went wrong, and also that the matter was being reported to the Chief Secretary.

I was stunned. At the dead of night, I had none else around me to be consulted or to discuss the matter.

The Commissioner then and there spoke to the Chief Secretary and told him about my disinclination to obey her verbal order. The Chief Secretary called me on the hotline and asked me as to what the problem was. I explained everything to the Chief Secretary and also submitted to him that it would be administratively wrong to cancel the passes. The Chief Secretary heard me patiently, and only asked me if I would be able to handle the situation in case of any problem. I replied in the affirmative, but put in a request for placing at my disposal whatever force that could be spared.

The Chief Secretary told me that he would be speaking to the IG concerned about force. The IG (Election Force) rang me himself and told me that he could only spare a posse of a hundred home guards. I thanked him.

As soon as I had finished my dialogues, I thought over the situation, somewhat dismayed. Of one thing I was sure that the Commissioner could only give me advice in election matters, as statutorily only the District Election Officer had the final responsibility. I thought that even if my decision was questioned, it would be an error on the right side and within my jurisdiction.

I then spoke to the SP without any gap of time and told him what had passed between me and the Commissioner. The SP, who was an officer of sagacity, asked me if I was going to stick to my decision as per book. I told him, I was not going to reconsider my decision of not cancelling the agents' counting passes. He told me that he would ensure that there was no problem and that he was quickly going to review the police arrangements without any loss of time.

The SP came to my residence at 6 a.m., and we discussed everything to make sure that the counting went on smoothly. We learnt that a huge crowd had already collected in front of Lohia College, Churu—the venue of counting.

Counting began as scheduled at 2 p.m. and lasted up to 6 a.m. the next day. Not a sparrow flew during this period. As per procedure, election certificates were issued to the winning candidates, and we all dispersed peacefully.

All this time, I had been keeping an eye over Bikaner affairs. There also, everything went on smoothly.

On hearing from me that in Churu district the counting went off peacefully, the Commissioner congratulated me for good performance. The nocturnal excitement was forgotten, and I was in my usual mental make-up. There was then no occasion to discuss this matter with the Commissioner or the Chief Secretary. I only thanked my stars and relaxed.

# 25

# Administrator as an Agent of Social Change

Rajendra Bhanawat

Dungarpur is a small district situated in the southern Rajasthan with a population of about a million. Two-third of the population is of tribals. Since most of the land is unirrigated, the district continues to be one of the most backward in the state. The rural habitation is such that the non-tribal population lives in a cluster form in the main village, whereas the tribals live in various hamlets. The terrain is quite hilly and undulating. The literacy percentage continues to be one of the lowest in the state. Due to low levels of literacy and development, there is a prevalence of a number of strange practices, one of which is the practice of *Mautana*. According to this, if a person dies in any house or village other than his own, his family claims an amount as a compensation death called *Mautana*. The presumption is that the family or the village where he had gone and dies is responsible for his death. The dead body of the person is not removed from the house unless *Mautana* is paid. Normally, a major part of the amount so paid is shared by the middle men or the self-imposed leaders of the community. This practice resulted into situations where the poor persons had to sell or mortgage their jewellery or properties or take loan to pay the amount to get rid of the dead body placed outside their house. The practice was so deep-rooted in a couple of blocks of the district that even the educated persons of the tribal community found it difficult to do anything about it.

I joined this district as Collector and District Magistrate in July 1995. Before I arrived in the district, whenever demand was raised as *Mautana*, the district administration always used to remain a silent spectator and the body continued to lie outside the house for days together. I was told that in one such incident it remained in such a condition for as many as nine days. Sometimes, the administration even played the role of an agent to finalise the *Mautana* amount. Although everyone including the members of the tribal community felt it was thoroughly unwarranted, none of them had the courage to take steps to stop this.

On 6 April 1996, in the evening when I was on tour in a small village, a wireless message was received that the dead body of Sarpanch Ramlal of Vikasnagar Panchayat had been kept in front of the house of the Upsarpanch of the same Panchayat, who belonged to a farming community, viz., Patidar. I was also informed that about 500 tribals had gathered outside the village in an aggressive mood. I immediately rushed to the site. Briefly the facts mentioned by the police were like this. Shri Ramlal Sarpanch, a tribal, was found unconscious near his scooter when he was going to his village from Dungarpur. The family members of Ramlal were informed and they took him to Ahmedabad for treatment as Dungarpur being a small town, did not have proper facilities. The police registered a case of accident. In spite of treatment at Ahmedabad, Ramlal did not survive and died on 5 April 1996. The body of Ramlal was brought to Vikasnagar for cremation. When the body was being taken for cremation, it was brought back to the village and kept outside the house of the Upsarpanch alleging that he was responsible for the death of Ramlal. It is relevant to mention here that the deceased Sarpanch and Upsarpanch belonged to two major political parties of the state.

On reaching Vikasnagar, I found a large crowd of tribals waiting for me, most of them with *lathis*. Their main demand was that Gehrilal Upsarpanch and his brothers be handed over to them as they were responsible for the murder of Ramlal. I explained to them that no FIR was there alleging this. If an FIR was made to the police, appropriate action would be taken to find out the guilty. I gave them some time to think and made it clear that dead body could not be allowed to remain outside the house. I also tried my best to convince them that their action was not only against law, but also against the Hindu customs, according to which, dead body must be cremated as per the rites. On the following two days, I consulted all relevant sections of society including the press, leaders of all political parties and senior officers. The local people including tribal leaders were of the view that such an evil practice must be put to an end. They also made it clear that Collector should have the courage to remove the dead body from the scene. If it was done, they would support. But none of them was willing to take the initiative. Meanwhile, the body started degenerating and smelling very foul, as it was summer time. The occupants of the house wanted to go to any other place as it was impossible to live in the house with a dead body in front of the gate. On 8 April, the Patidar women laid themselves down in front of my car when I went to the village, demanding immediate removal of dead body so that they could live normally. For two days, I kept on persuading the tribal middlemen to remove the body from the house. It is worth mentioning here that the survivors of the deceased were sensible persons but they were overpowered by the so-called local community chieftains. In spite of the advice of the police, not to go in the midst of the crowd of tribals, I did so as I had full trust in residents of my district. I knew that they were very simple people who were being misled. When I told them about the action taken by police on their FIR, they were not interested and changed their stand. They agreed that no punishment could be given to Gehrilal, as there was no evidence and the case was weak. But they then raised a demand for payment of ₹ 51 lakh as *Mautana*, failing which they would cremate the body in front of Gehrilal's house and burn all houses of Patidars. It may be mentioned that the basis of allegation of murder was the so-called utterance of the deceased just before death that Gehrilal was responsible for it. The situation was very sensitive on the following grounds:

(a) The parties involved were tribals and non-tribals respectively.

(b) The Patidars had asked their contacts at other places to come to the village. This could have led to a caste war in the district.

(c) The Lok Sabha elections were scheduled for 27 April 1996.

When all efforts of persuasion failed, we decided to act irrespective of the consequences. I said to myself that district administration would no longer be a silent spectator. After convincing all concerned of my proposed action, as SP was reluctant in taking the stern steps of removing the body from the site, I requested DIG, Udaipur, in the night of 8 April 1996. Proper police arrangements were made.

We all reached Vikasnagar at 4 a.m. on 9 April 1996, got the body removed and sent it to mortuary at Dungarpur. A few persons were apprehended also. As expected, with the dawn, the drums started beating. It may be mentioned here that drum-beating is a fool-proof system of communication to members of the tribal community. Various rhythms of drum beats are used in different situations. This was an emergency signal to community to gather. The drum beating went on incessantly for hours. By evening, more than 3,000 tribals had gathered outside the village shouting slogans against the administration and the Patidars. Some middlemen came to meet us to help them in getting ₹ 51 lakh from Patidars. We were firm in approach that we would not become party to such an evil and arbitrary practice. They started advancing towards the village to attack it. They started throwing stones by 'Gofans'—an indigenous instrument which throws stone like a bullet.

Soon after, they put the grain storage on fire. The Patidars became panicky and wanted to come out to fight the tribals. The warning by police to disperse did not have any effect and the crowd continued with its burning and stoning activity. The teargas shells and lathi charge were resorted, but no avail as anticipated. The tribals were on hills all around and these methods had no effect on them. I, along with DIG, was on one front, whereas SP and SDM on the other. Suddenly, sound of firing was heard. In fact, we wanted to avoid firing, specially in view of the imminent parliamentary elections. Shouting stopped and the gathering dispersed. The SP and SDM informed us later that firing had become essential to save villagers and the police force from attack by tribals.

Our immediate task was to find out the outcome of firing. Message came from police chowki that three persons had been seriously injured. When we wanted to shift them to Dungarpur hospital, we came to know that during the day, road from Dungarpur had been badly damaged and no vehicle could go. Therefore, they had to go by a very long route, which was 70 km instead of direct one, which was only 15 km.

When they reached Dungarpur hospital at about 11 p.m., wireless message was received by me that one of the injured needed blood, without which, he was likely to collapse on way to Udaipur hospital. We were in the village, but by that time, news about firing on tribals had reached the state headquarter and continuous phone calls started pouring in. All arrangements for treatment at hospital Udaipur had been fixed from Jaipur, but the main problem was of arranging blood immediately, to keep them alive, till the patient reached Udaipur. The problem was serious as there was no blood bank at Dungarpur. It was here that my wife played a very crucial role. She immediately got in touch with the secretary of the local branch of Mahaveer International, who she had known at a social function. He went to the hospital and donated blood himself as the blood group matched incidentally. Subsequently, after treatment at Udaipur, all the injured survived.

The following day, i.e., 10 April 1996, Divisional Commissioner from Udaipur and IG from Jaipur also arrived. The Chief Minister sent a minister to the site along with other local politicians.

Though the law and order problem had been contained, the major task was still before us, i.e., the disposal of the dead body lying in the mortuary at Dungarpur. We were aware that disposal of the body by the police without consent of deceased's family could lead to grave consequences, especially in view of the ensuing elections. The politicians were apprised of the situation and were persuaded to convince the family of deceased to accept the body and cremate it according to their customs. Initially, no result seemed to be forthcoming, but ultimately, after a series of dialogues, the family members of the deceased agreed to receive the body in the evening. Immediately, the body was brought back to Vikasnagar and handed over to the family. The police was asked to remain present at the site of cremation to guard against any possibility of change of mind. At around midnight, we were informed that the cremation had taken place without any problem. All of us heaved a sigh of relief.

The following points regarding the episode need to be mentioned here:

(a) Though the firing was the main front page news in all state-level newspapers, nowhere it was reported that it was unwarranted or unnecessary.

(b) No section of the local society, including the political parties, most of whose leaders were tribals said anything against it.

(c) This was probably the first incident of firing in Dungarpur since independence.

(d) The parliamentary elections, which were held only about a fortnight after this incident, were extremely peaceful and normal. Even the polling percentage was the same, as in other parts of the state.

(e) On the day of firing, it appeared to me for a moment that my communication with tribals would come to an end, but it was very heartening to note that their respect for and trust in me had increased tremendously.

(f) For the first time, dead body from outside the house of another person was removed without payment of any *Mautana* and without involvement of any middlemen.

(g) An evil practice of blackmailing poor tribals and other poor persons had ultimately been put to an end. It was well endorsed by another incident after about a month when dead body though kept outside the house of a Rajput was lifted by tribals themselves within two hours.

(h) The efforts to persuade the family members to accept the body succeeded in spite of firing.

We learnt several lessons from this social barrier breaking episode. The administration should in no case feel helpless. It must always be prepared to show its effectiveness specially for a good social cause. The issue of social change should be seen not only from the law and order point of view, but also from social angles and implications. For example, handing over body to the family was a major decision, which was implemented successfully.

We should take all segments of population into confidence. People are willing to support an action of the administration, if it enjoys the basic trust of the people. We should never be afraid of meeting and mixing freely with common men of the district. Non-communication is the basic cause of distrust between the people and the administration. Even the family of a District Magistrate has to play a role sometimes. If they are prepared for it, they will be able to do so more effectively.

# Part II

## Cherishable Memories

# 26

# S.L. Khurana

## A Colossus

I.C. Srivastava

Sundar Lal Khurana, the first IAS recruit to be allotted to Rajasthan cadre who rose to be the state's Chief Secretary and later Union Home Secretary and Governor of Tamil Nadu, inspired awe and admiration at the same time. He strode like colossus not only in bureaucratic set up during his tenure as Chief Secretary but also called the shots for MLAs and politicians of Rajasthan on behalf of Barkutullah Khan, the then Chief Minister who had full faith in his sagacity, acumen and wisdom. It may be recalled that M.L. Sukhadia, the longest serving Chief Minister was made to resign by the then Prime Minister Mrs Indira Gandhi early in 1971 and was replaced by Barkutullah Khan, an otherwise amiable and admirable person but a comparatively junior Minister in charge only of Law and Justice. It was widely believed in bureaucratic parlance that Khurana's appointment as Chief Secretary was also approved by Indira Gandhi whose confidence he seemed to enjoy as it was later reflected in his conduct of state affairs on his own and in his own style according to the need of the situation in the wakc of ongoing Bangladesh freedom struggle. Though short in height, his stocky and sturdy physical appearance and penetrating eyes more often overawed almost everyone who came in official contact with him. His gurgling high-pitched voice lent weight to his dominating personality. In meetings and conferences, his thundering inaugural speech and terrifying tone held the audience captive and speechless most of the time.

In the annual Senior Officers' Conference attended by Collectors and Heads of Departments, he was at his glorious best. Chief Minister, Khan, after his brief inaugural speech which, in part, eulogised Khurana's abilities and acumen in administrative matters would sit back relaxed alongwith his ministers among whom few would interject or intervene in discussions. Khurana would hold forth himself as he warmed up and occasionally snub or admonish the senior officers like an old headmaster with baton, his lashing tongue replacing the baton. When in command, he would not spare the seniormost if an occasion arose. One of his famous and seething remarks that government was not expected to consult a Head of the Department on all matters concerning him set the tone and tenor of discussions, though it certainly made the then Chairman of Board of Revenue his own batchmate fret and fume in his close by seat. In the Regional Conference at Jodhpur in 1972, the then Director of Agriculture was snubbed and chided like a child for his unguarded remark in a press conference that the state was in the midst of the worst famine not witnessed for several decades. Thenceforth, no Head of the Department would venture to talk to the press without full preparation and government clearance of facts.

Khurana was also jovial and humorous when occasion demanded. His wit and humour then resounded the hall and participants would breathe easy and joined him in his spontaneous laughter. He was vivacious and bubbling with energy all the time. His all pervading power and awesome personality made such a great impact on the political heat and dust of times that all matters including political ones faced by the administration were settled with grace and ease under his benign influence. His command over state affairs sent out positive vibrations throughout the state during the year 1971 when war with Pakistan seemed not only imminent but also loomed large on the horizon. The state administration, therefore, under his inimitable administrative leadership geared itself to the preparations of war in necessary coordination with army and air force at all levels.

I was then posted as Collector and District Magistrate of border district of Barmer, one of the largest in the country. The Shimla Agreement of 1972 provided, among other things, that the territory occupied by the defence forces on both sides during the war should be returned to the respective countries. An agitation was launched in July–August 1972 by the Bharatiya Jana Sangh (BJS), a prominent opposition political party against this provision of the agreement. I was recalled from leave, and thus I travelled back in 103°F temperature from Udaipur to my district headquarters just three days before the opposition leader concerned and his followers arrived at Barmer.

In accordance with the announcement made by Shri A.B. Vajpayee, the leader of the opposition party, the agitation was initially planned at various important places all along 250 km of the international boundary of Barmer district. However, Gadra road railway station located near the international border and about 100 km from Barmer district headquarters became the focal point of this agitation. From here, the opposition leader was going to launch the agitation and set its tone and pace. Also from here, the agitators were to enter the 'occupied area' on way to Gadra City situated about 10 kms inside the Pakistan territory then under control of our army. The agitators decided to camp at Gadra road railway station. The agitation created an unprecedented situation for us.

It would be recalled that the largest chunk of Pakistan territory, about 8,000 sq km in area, which was occupied by the Indian Army included two tehsil headquarter townships Chachro and Nagarparkar of Tharparker district of Pakistan. After the war, early in 1972, the then Chief Minister of Rajasthan, had gone to Chachro and unfurled the Indian national flag signifying that the area was not only under our occupation but it was also to be administered by civil administration of the state. It was not clear then that the territory would be returned to Pakistan.

On the first day, at about 9 a.m. Shri Atal Behari Vajpayee, the agitation leader led a procession of more than 200 volunteers including some women volunteers who had come all the way from Maharashtra. The procession was, as usual, escorted by a posse of police force. All the senior officers followed the agitators and watched them cross the international boundary line. The volunteers marched ahead with gusto and fanfare. On reaching Gadra city in 'occupied area', they had to perforce camp in a Krishna temple which was the only pucca structure in that village.

When it came to crunch, we faced the agitation squarely. According to the guidelines received from the state government, the agitators were to be released by the concerned Magistrate under Sec. 62 Cr. PC as they had committed no offence on the Indian territory. Briefly, the strategy was that the agitators should be let off so that they were forced to return home at their own expense, or if they so desired, they could stay on and continue the agitation. As the agitators were expecting to be arrested and sent to various jails before being released, they were almost shocked by our action. Much to our relief, the agitation received an immediate setback.

The opposition leader was almost stunned as he slumped on the only cot placed on railway platform at Gadra road station. He expressed his great consternation to me when I told him that he and his followers were being released immediately after the army had formally handed them over to us. The batch of volunteers who had come all the way on the first day were asked to stay on for the next few days to carry on the agitation. The leader himself stayed on to plan his next move. As the agitation was likely to fizzle out, the agitators got it circulated that a 'dharana' would be staged at the railway station and on the rail tracks both at Barmer and Gadra road in order to dislocate the movement of trains. This created a new set of problems for us.

After hurried consultations, it was decided that if found necessary, force should be used for the removal of volunteers from railway stations and rail tracks. I also discussed this matter on telephone with Shri Khurana, the then Chief Secretary who immediately gave me a green signal for taking such strong action as might be warranted by the situation besides adding a word of encouragement for the proper handling of the agitation until then. The agitators probably got scent of the proposed strong action and, therefore, did not finally stage the proposed dharana.

The drama of marching processions into the 'occupied' territory continued for almost 3 weeks. But the opposition leader left the district after six days, leaving a handful of agitators to register their protest every day by enacting the melodrama. The agitation, as expected, started petering out even before coming to an unsung finale.

My posting at Jaipur as Administrator of Cooperative Marketing Federation (RKVSS) in September 1972 after the tumultuous and hectic preoccupation with Indo-Pak War 1971 (Experience narrated in 'Battle Cry' essay included in the author's book *Challenge and Change in Administrative System*) and Pak refugee relief gruelling task came as a welcome relief to me and my family. But soon enough, I was catapulted to State Secretariat as Deputy Secretary in January 1973. While I was still grappling to find my moorings in Secretariat work, in November 1973, I received a phone call directly from Khurana at Udaipur where I had gone to see my father who was undergoing treatment at a hospital. Khurana's loud and clear, resonating voice came as a big surprise to me as a junior officer, 'Srivastava, I learn that your father is not well and hospitalised at Udaipur. I have this post of Director, Rehabilitation, Kadana and Mahi Projects, lying vacant at Banswara which is not far from Udaipur. I suggest, you take this so that you will be close to your parents and family as well', What could I say except replying 'Yes, Sir'. From Barmer where I had worked in the tumultuous war times and its aftermath to my great satisfaction and with some distinction and honour on having received merit and commendation letter from Chief Secretary himself to two postings at Jaipur as aforesaid were a welcome change. However, within 14 months this was the third assignment. Its experience I did not regret at all, and it became the subject of my essay titled 'The Belated Agreement' in the book as aforesaid. At that point of time, I had mixed feelings about shaping my career under the wayward wings of government 'adhoc(ism)' or non-chalant approach to career planning of officers, which has done much harm to the state cadre comparatively at the all India level. But in retrospect, one can also derive some satisfaction from the fact that those were the times when Chief Secretary used to informally sound officers before posting them anyway so as to keep up their morale on frequent transfers. Times have changed. Manipulations and machinations are the names of the games for most of the officers. Others suffer in sulking silence and bide their time to do the same in their turn. Few upright ones do well on their own and lend charm and grace to any assignment despite all pulls and pressures. They make their own way up or exit scintillating without blame or blemish.

Before I end this narrative tribute to Khurana, the great administrator, I would like to recall and record a personal trait that may complete the portrait I have drawn. Khurana's all out support and backing to Collectors of four border districts—Barmer, Bikaner, Jaisalmer and Sri Ganganagar during, before and after Indo-Pak War—had resulted into successful civil defence arrangements, and other preparatory work in run up to the outbreak of war in December 1971 besides necessary coordination with army and air force set up at various levels. But he was dismayed, nay probably disappointed in not being able to secure 'Padma Shri' award to the border district Collectors. The army having an upper hand in processing war awards went ahead without consulting the state government whereby Shri Vijay Singh, Collector and District Magistrate, Sri Ganganagar alone was awarded Padma Shri. Later it was revealed that Collectors of all other border districts of the country were conferred this award. When the state government sent the recommendations it was rather late as the Government of India had not only taken decision in this regard but also made the announcement in which only one Collector figured as aforesaid. But before this happened, little realising that Government of India would not consider another set of recommendations of the state government, Khurana vibrant with grace and charm invited me to see him in his office on my way back to Barmer on completion of my leave. When I called on him, with his usual verve and vivacity he disclosed that my name alongwith others had been recommended for Padma Shri award and I could expect the same as soon as possible. Here was a man, confident of his action and the result thereof, who could inspire confidence and high morale among service officers by real esprit de corps. But probably he could not turn the tide of events in his favour and remained inconsolate in this regard. However, as Union Home Secretary his work and achievements during Emergency Rule in the country is part of nation's history. His personae remains enshrined and etched in our memory. He will be long remembered as a great administrative leader.

# 27

# Mohan Mukerji

I.C. Srivastava

One of the most distinguished civil servants of Rajasthan, Mohan Mukerji held several posts with distinction, including those of Development Commissioner, Finance Secretary and finally Chief Secretary, Government of Rajasthan for which he was recalled from his assignment of Additional Secretary, Culture, under Government of India. Uniquely for any officer, he served as Collector of Ajmer district twice, which experience not only gave a fillip to his creative mind but also stood him in good stead throughout his brilliant administrative career. Although I had met him briefly in September 1972 as Administrator of Rajasthan Cooperative Market Federation, on my transfer back to Jaipur from my first district assignment of Barmer, I had the good fortune of working directly under him as Deputy Secretary, GAD and Cabinet in 1975–1976 during 'Emergency' period when he was at his scintillating best as Chief Secretary.

I can vividly recall quite a few memorable meetings with him because in routine matters however important they might be, he had delegated to me his own powers under rules unless I felt constrained for some reason to seek his guidance urgently or otherwise. One such instance can be easily narrated to indicate clearly his sharp intellect, pragmatic approach and a keen desire to find instant solutions especially to politico-cum-protocol issues. This episode relates to the well-publicised, high-profile visit of Sanjay Gandhi to Bikaner early in 1976. The VVIP treatment he had received a few days earlier in Haryana had put senior police officers on alert and alarm. Even curious rural crowd was expected to turn up in large numbers to attend the public meeting scheduled to be addressed by him with his newfound 'mantra'— 'Baatain Kam Kaam Jyada'. He had already begun to be addressed as the new leader of young India and had become an icon for the surging crowds.

Briefly, the security issues for the State Police CID were reduced to two demands made to GAD: provision of two white Ambassador cars from the State Garage and a temporary telephone connection below the rostrum generally provided for Prime Minister on official visit. Being Deputy Secretary of General Administration Department (GAD), I also functioned ex-officio as State Protocol Officer and in that capacity I was required to maintain and observe protocol. For the Youth Congress leader that he was, there was no priority in the order of precedence or the State Guest list of dignitaries. In fact his position did not figure in the central list too. When the then DIG, CID, rang up as a follow-up to the letter of requisition for two cars and a temporary telephone as aforesaid, my initial reaction was a point blank 'no'. But the then IGP, Ganesh Singh also tried to contact me. Little realising how to duck the issue, I made myself unavailable for a while. But Mr O.P. Tandon, DIG, came to Secretariat personally looking for my location. I, then, decided to seek the guidance from the Chief Secretary, Mukerji, who was also ex-officio Secretary, GAD. As he could be available at 6 p.m., I requested Shri Tandon to contact me at 6.30 p.m. on the eve of the so-called VVIPs' visit. Mukerji, a highly experienced bureaucrat found an easy administrative solution to a politico-cum-protocol problem, way out for which could not be found at my level.

'Yes, Srivastava. What is it that is bothering you?', he asked me.

On my explaining to him the problem as precisely and briefly as possible, he exclaimed, 'It is not a big problem. You see, the Police Department has sent you the requisition. Allot to Police Department vehicles as well as temporary telephone for security duties. While the vehicles will be on security deployment, Police Department will be responsible for paying the bills to Telephone

Department for installation and call charges of telephone, from their own budget, as GAD only allots telephones even otherwise'.

What a great relief it was to me to have found a quick solution to a troublesome problem!

Mukerji had enjoyed, as Finance Secretary, an enviable reputation of being a Finance wizard with his long tenure and practical ways to explore and discover solutions to varied emerging issues especially in state's fast industrialisation process. Being suave and forthcoming as a gentle but clear-headed conversationalist, he could carry conviction with political masters across the political divide. Besides, enjoying as he did the full confidence of the then Chief Minister, M.L. Sukhadia, and later H.D. Joshi, he never minced words when it came to crunch without raising his voice or tone. Though seniormost, he would always put his colleagues and subordinates at ease unlike his illustrious and awesome predecessor, S.L. Khurana. Inclined to groom his officers in their career, Mukerji had a sensitive personae, full of compassion and empathy, which trickled and showed in genial flow of his thoughts and ideas for others. Thus, he sent a newly recruited, young woman tourist officer for training to Vienna even though service rules did not permit this. He could probably envision her budding career for which such a training opportunity could not be missed. The officer on return from training was immediately assigned duties as protocol officer to escort Indira Gandhi, the then Prime Minister on her historic trip to Haldighati on the 21st June 1976. Nobody but Mukerji alone could foresee such a role for that officer.

While on the subject of training, when I received a message to forward my 'resume' for training in UK under Colombo Plan as Deputy Secretary, Tourism, a job included in my position as DS GAD, he asked me to come over to his residence where he found time to guide me to prepare a write-up to do something extra during training, i.e., to study local administration there. This opportunity I had to miss due to one Ms. Baal then working in Ministry of Tourism who managed to wangle it. But Mukerji's caring and grooming nature is still etched clearly in my memory.

Let me recall another example of his compassionate interpersonal relationship. When I applied for a government accommodation, my section officer in GAD showed me the rule that a Deputy Secretary could not be allotted, out-of-turn, any government accommodation. But as required by Rules of Business, he took the file without routing it through me, directly to Mukerji, Chief Secretary being Secretary GAD as well. Mr Mukerji in his imitable manner noted on the file that DS GAD who also worked as Head of the Department for Motor Garage and Circuit Houses was entitled for out-of-turn allotment, adding for good measure that Srivastava would not be allotted any house in Jaipur in future once Rajasthan Housing Board allotted him a house against his pending application. A bungalow was allotted in no time, but we could live there only for 10 months.

In August 1976, I was posted out as Collector, Ganganagar. It was an unpleasant surprise to me to receive these posting orders in Secretariat dak. I immediately rushed to Chief Secretary's chamber. He was busy with his files. In sheer anger and with pent up feelings, I could not resist telling him that if I had displeased him on something or if he was dissatisfied with my work, he could have told me before issuing orders. He burst into laughter and gave his own explanation. Government wanted a person of my seniority and experience to go as Collector, Sri Ganganagar. Besides, my wife being a botanist would enjoy and also maintain the lovely rose garden in Collector's residence. What could I say? Of course, he was cool and patient enough to listen to and appreciate a young officer's problem of moving with family at short notice. Mukerji being an amiable person to the core, I could not think of saying anything more. Needless to add, my experience in Ganganagar became memorable and extremely useful in many ways especially in developing interpersonal relationships which have lasted as a family until my post-retirement period.

However, with a quirk of circumstance, after the defeat in Parliamentary Elections of March 1977, I was again brought back to Jaipur as Director, Small Savings & Lotteries, in May 1977 as Family Welfare Camps (or Nasbandi camps as they were called) were still continuing in the district, and the then CM apprehended that if I continued there it might be one of the reasons why the ruling party was likely to lose in State Assembly Elections in June 1977 as well. But strange are the ways of God and Government! The ruling

Congress Party did lose the Assembly Elections and somehow, the new Janata Party Government decided, in July 1977, to post me as Collector Bharatpur where I had started my career as SDO/SDM Bharatpur in 1968. With some reluctance which was overcome with persuasion by the new CM, B.S. Shekhawat and the then Finance Minister, Master Adityendra, I arrived by the last train at Bharatpur before the city was surrounded by swirling flood waters on three sides including railway tracks. This short narration here has become necessary to complete my impressions and picture of Mukerji, one of the tallest and most admired administrators of Rajasthan state.

With Emergency over, the day of superannuation was drawing closer for Mukerji. In the last week of October 1977, I got a call from my first friend in service, Anil Kumar (1965 batch IAS) to travel with family in my private car to Jaipur to bid farewell to our esteemed leader and the first civil servant. At the behest of IAS Association, it was conveyed to us in the districts that this farewell function would be totally unofficial and contributory, of course. However, a post-Emergency backlash did not diminish esprit de corp nor did it lower our morale for we had worked under Emergency with little or no excesses and no stigma attached to any one of us with one or two exceptions which always proved the rule.

The fond farewell function held in the congenial Sisodia Rani Garden generated our enthusiasm to the core. Songs from service officers and family members were interspersed with tales and humorous anecdotes mostly by seniors. Mukerji with his characteristic wit and humour related why he preferred to pen his signature in English for some time despite government instructions to switch over to signature in 'Hindi' until he learnt to correct his erroneous Hindi spelling of Moorkhji to Mukerji. What a hilarious laughter this remark aroused can be recalled with nostalgia by those who were present there and only imagined by others who were not. To top it all, we witnessed the fondest ever farewell to him and his gracious wife Reena. They were a graceful, winsome and charming couple all their life and were always remembered as such by all those who came to know him as a colleague or as a member of Jaipur gentry, politicians included. Therefore, when we received in 1988 the saddest and most shocking news of their sudden demise in a road accident in West Germany, we were dumbfounded for a while in disbelief and grief before realisation of losing both of them to destiny on their way to heavenly abode. At his house, Shyamoli located at Rambagh Circle, we witnessed with tears the lowering of their coffins for a prayer meeting in which their daughter, Malashree Lal read out her emotionally charged and well-worded, almost poetic speech which still seems to ring a bell of reverence and homage in our hearts for the dear departed souls, may be, now shining stars in the firmament.

# 28

# G.K. Bhanot

I.C. Srivastava

Gopal Krishna Bhanot, the first direct recruit IAS Officer (1949 batch) of the state was the only officer to have served as Chief Secretary twice; earlier in the then Union Territory of Goa, Daman & Diu and later in Rajasthan (1977–1980). A person with no-nonsense and clear-headed approach on problems—personal state or public, Bhanot was appointed Chief Secretary in the aftermath of Emergency by the Janata Party. In fact, one day he confided in his post-retirement and past siesta conversation that the newly elected CM had come to his residence to 'invite' (nay request) him to take over as the Chief Secretary which he not only accepted but also justified the confidence reposed in him with distinction, equanimity and neutrality—the hallmark of that office. Held in high esteem by colleagues and subordinates down various echelons of administration, he maintained and displayed a strict exterior and demeanour in official matters but was compassionate to the core and deeply empathetic in heart when he happened to discuss personal problems of junior officers. Impartial, free and frank advice to government not only in files but during discussions as well with political masters were the characteristics, which he wanted to inculcate among officers who came in contact with him.

Busy as he was during day time in various meetings, receiving visitors and hearing complaints and officers' grievances, he found time, one wondered how, to dispose off almost all his files every day before going home. At home, he felt relaxed and put at ease others who called on him. Occasionally, he would organise some music recital or Ghazal evening at home for which he invited those who were not only inclined to listen to good music but could also appreciate the same. He himself was fond of singing Ghazals and sang duets with his wife Prema besides playing on harmonium. Needless to add, such occasions, though rare, were eagerly awaited by the interested ones.

Posted in the district, we could only visit his place for a call on. As I had reluctantly taken over as Collector, Bharatpur, in August 1977 and having been transferred thrice in past one year, I did not anticipate a fourth transfer within a year after all the hard work put in during floods, and Revenue Campaign and Panchayat elections coming my way one after the other. But powers that be always face the challenge of remaining in power and the constraint of removing straightforward unbending officer even though he had been persuaded or forced to join a few months back. Even so, a healing touch was applied by Shri Bhanot who called me to Jaipur not only to sound me on my transfer in the offing but also to soothe my frayed nerves. If I recall correctly, he said, 'You have done extremely well. I am fully satisfied with your work but you know the person, the local MP who is hell bent on your transfer for reasons well-known to you. But I am sending you to Udaipur as Excise Commissioner, which is a very important assignment for your age and seniority. Also, you would be with your parents and brothers' families there'. Chief Secretary's call to meet him and disclosure of his mind to a junior officer about his constraints were enough to soothe my nerves. What else could one think of the head of the Civil Service who minced no words to make 'the situation clear and also gave a pat to encourage me in my career ahead'.

The local MP had approached me with a list of transfers of employees, which he wanted to be issued. My promise to get the proposals examined did not cut much ice with him. During Emergency, he had joined the Janata Party bandwagon alongwith his 'red cap' socialist followers. Having spent a number of months as a jail inmate with the newly-elected CM during Emergency period detention under MISA Act, he thought he could prevail upon him to transfer me at the earliest. I had got an inkling of his putting pressure on CM for this purpose. Meanwhile, I was called by Shri Bhanot to discuss all this. Mentally prepared as I was to move, I decided to go on my first well-earned LTC with family. As a family, we travelled during December 1977–January 1978 for a fortnight in South India via Bombay, Pune and Goa, and enjoyed the trip thoroughly before my resuming back to duties at Bharatpur.

Eventually, I was transferred as Excise Commissioner Udaipur in May 1978. I could hardly remain at Udaipur for five months and large family reunion with my brothers, their children and my parents was, to their great dismay and our frustration, short-lived though lively, nostalgic and full of joy. Thus, my next posting as Secretary to the then Governor, Raghukul Tilak was unbelievably dramatic. However, the manipulative behind-the-scene-drama was revealed to me only after I was forced to join at Governor's Secretariat and that too with His Excellency's approval in an interview organized at his SMS Hospital bedside. In sequence, three officers managed to wriggle out of this unenviable position as they were lucky enough to be supported by their powerful bureaucrat bosses while my immediate supervisory officer was merely a Special Secretary in the Finance Department.

In retrospect, I feel my family enjoyed my Raj Bhawan tenure more than me, only partly relaxed as it was for a working-type officer. I was advised by Shri Bhanot (who was already sympathetic but probably found himself helpless in deference to HE's choice) to take my work in a relaxed mode. The facility of tennis Club at Raj Bhawan was, however, a redeeming feature for me besides the library well stocked with books of choice, ranging from Governor's household demands to catering to children's needs and taste. Freedom from Raj Bawan came to me in the form of orders of deputation to Government of India. I received orders of my assignment as Director, Census Operations, for Rajasthan State under Ministry of Home Affairs with headquarters at Jaipur while I was receiving training under Advanced Management Development Programme at Mussoorie in June 1979. On my arrival at Jaipur, I was congratulated by my friends for my selection by GoI to head the decennial census work of 1981. It turned out to be an academic and an 'innocuous' task lasting for four years during which a 9-month training programme at

Manchester University (UK) under Colombo Plan in Development Administration from September 1981 to June 1982 acted as a morale booster after going through the travail of five transfers in a span of 18 months. My 4-year tenure as Director, Census, unique in many ways proved to be a most fruitful period of prolific and productive endeavours for me in having to edit more than 40 volumes of Census publications which included special studies of certain villages, towns, tribes and crafts as well, to my great satisfaction.

I received full support from G.K. Bhanot—the then Chief Secretary who took no time in issuing a circular to all the Secretaries to the Government of Rajasthan, Collectors and Heads of Departments, enjoining them to extend all possible help and cooperation to the Directorate in the conduct of census operations besides according the same priority and treatment to the correspondence and instructions issued by the Directorate as was given to state government orders. When I called on him as Director of Census Operations, his first remarks were, 'I have already signed all the three circulars which you requested for, yesterday evening; what else would you like me to do?' It came to me as a very pleasant surprise as I had gone to see him only to explain the need for the issue of the three circulars in question. It was immensely satisfying to find that they had already been signed by the seniormost and busiest officer of the state within 24 hours of my request. The Chief Secretary's circular helped not only in gearing up the administrative machinery at various levels but also in setting up the hierarchy of functionaries for control and supervision.

However, 2–3 months before population count (February to March 1981), Bhanot was transferred and posted as Chairman, Board of Revenue, which position though equivalent in pay and rank to Chief Secretary, appeared to be a 'comedown' in public eye for a serving Chief Secretary. Although M.M.K. Wali, his successor fully supported me in my work besides releasing the booklet, *Provisional Population Totals of 1981 Census*, in a press Conference addressed jointly by him and the author, I greatly missed the informal, relaxed ambience of Bhanot and his chamber where he inspired confidence and trust in officers by his inimitable conversational style at times interspersed with his paan (betel) chewing exercise.

Of course, I was lucky alongwith three other colleagues to get another opportunity of working with Bhanot at Board of Revenue, Ajmer, where I was posted on promotion in 1983. It came as a surprise to me to observe Bhanot's changed style of administration as Chairman. Besides sitting regularly in the Court, he would discuss the complicated revenue cases in his chamber with member colleagues especially with the new arrivals like me to provide so-to-say necessary grooming and orientation. Needless to add, the grooming by him and grinding work itself added to our clarity of thought, precision in expression and rural perspective in outlook all of which stood us in good stead in the later years of our career. Bhanot's chamber lectures on Saturdays, which also became discussion session for an hour or so went a long way in improving the quality and value of our judgements some of which were reported in Revenue Law Journal called *Rajasthan Revenue Decisions (RRD).*

Last but not least, how can I forget his gesture of directing me to go on privilege leave (PL) for a month to prepare myself for ensuing LLB Final Exams in April 1984, even if the target of my cases might not be achieved during that period. He, somehow, came to know of my studying for LLB course at home alongwith my official work of hearing cases and writing judgements and called me to his chamber. Before I could sit down, he burst forth, laughing, 'Srivastava, I learn, you are appearing at LLB Exam next month. I am indeed happy that you thought of adding to your knowledge and qualification'. But on my nod and some remarks he blurted. 'At this stage, you cannot manage both court work and your studies at the same time. I, therefore, suggest and would like you to take a month's leave so that you can do justice to your studies'. Needless to add, his advice was complied with. What a remarkable and endearing personality he was, one could make out only after coming and working in close contact with him.

His earmarked house at Ajmer buzzed with musical evenings organised by him occasionally to entertain colleagues on festivals or even otherwise. Ghazal singers from Hyderabad and other towns, who were on a visit to Khwaja Saheb Ki Dargah were invited by him to his house where they regaled all colleagues and others with their families until late in the night. Unforgettable days as they were, memory lingers as I look back with nostalgia, to those evenings when time stood apparently to the ennobling and elevating music, 'the food of love' and soul of life.

All in all, a hard task master, Mr Bhanot was an epitome of an admirable administrator with the gentleness and humility of a thorough gentleman at heart. A fine example of his care and concern for his junior colleagues was unveiled in my case when I received orders of my transfer as Secretary to Governor in May 1984 within 10 months of my posting as Member, Board of Revenue at Ajmer, which was considered an unenviable and 'punishment posting' for many. I had settled down to the non-administrative court work, and it could be reasonably expected that I would stay there at least for two years. Bhanot had remarked to a senior colleague in my absence that my performance was quite up to his expectations.

Transfer back to Jaipur, especially in the given situation that house was rented out and my children were receiving good education at Ajmer, was not only an unexpected and undesirable event but administratively unwarranted as well for an IAS officer, exception apart, is generally not posted to man the same position least of all as Secretary to Governor Mr Bhanot knew my situation and dilemma and therefore called for me to advise that I should call on the then Chief Secretary, Shri A.M. Lal to apprise him of my problem and viewpoint. Mr Lal, with his awesome physique and fierce looking eyes, inspired fear bordering on terror. Nonetheless encouraged and prompted by Shri Bhanot. I took courage and sought an appointment. Shri Lal blusted out, 'Srivastava, you don't want to come back to Jaipur from Board of Revenue how is that?'

On my explaining at length my situation and dilemmas as aforesaid, he softened, 'I did not realize it is going to be your second tenure as Secretary to Governor. But now I cannot cancel or change government orders. But I shall keep in mind. Don't worry too much. With lock, stock and barrel I came back to Jaipur in Raj Bhawan guest house with family and for a month or so I stayed with my family at Mt Abu in the earmarked house on Governor's insistence to treat us as his guest there which was an emotional appeal if not blackmail (under rules, Governor could not treat his Secretary and family as his official guests). Needless to add, that trip to Mt Abu was enjoyable and rejuvenating to our depressed spirits. The then Governor, Air Marshal Shri O.P. Mehra came to know about my disinterested, though efficient, performance in work as I had told him everything on our first meeting. To my great satisfaction and pleasant surprise, Mr A.M. Lal not only kept his promise but assigned me to the position of Secretary, Tourism, Culture and Sports a tenure of which I have cherished rich memories.

Summing up, I still look upon Shri Bhanot as a model administrator—down to earth in approach with a pulse on the people's problems and felt needs and a long-term vision of the state's progress and future without losing human touch anytime and in any situation.

# 29

# Yatindra Singh

## A Gentleman Par Excellence

**I.C. Srivastava**

Everyone, at least in the IAS cadre in Rajasthan and in his own circle of friends called him 'Yati' or 'Yatida'—'dada'—as it would suit the age and relationship—official or unofficial—of the person with him. Suave, soft-spoken and gentle as he was in his speech and gestures while interacting with anyone of any age group, he instantly made friends with service juniors and their children—for the latter he was a favourite friend and uncle. He always took care of others' needs and interests without expecting anything in return. In most cases, he intuitively knew what nudge or buzz would echo the right question or response for which he would find easy and feasible solutions. He would, for instance, suggest how one could seek and admit children to a good school or where one could buy good grocery items. For juniors arriving first time in capital, he would arrange rooms in circuit house and suggest good areas for rented accommodation as a government quarter was not available to Deputy Secretaries on priority. Once in a while, he would invite them at home and some seniors too not only to introduce the 'new arrivals' in the cadre to other colleagues but also to develop necessary camraderie and bonhomie. Children in teens would be taken out to picnic or trekking in Jhalana hills. This is how he became an uncle for all seasons for my own children. Being a sportsman, he would carry his tennis racket and kit in his car early in morning and more often than not after his usual game at Jai Club he would drive straight to the Secretariat. His flair to encourage colleagues to play games would also prompt him to lend his game kit to responsive ones. As he lent me half his golf kit, I could fairly guess how keen he was to shape the personality of the juniors on the right lines.

Discussing any subject—personal, official or even private ones—was a pleasurable intellectual exercise for him as he would be able to draw out the best ideas in such an ineffable, informal and affectionate manner that one would tend to lose the 'how and why' of a conversation for a while until, on introspection, one would correlate the reason which was only to groom the person or nudge him on the right track or direction in work or life.

As a probationer and trainee officer, my first pleasant encounter with him was early in the morning when I saw him bending over the bonnet of his official Ambassador car which had a breakdown in or around Ajmer at night on way to Jaipur from Bhilwara where he was posted as Collector and District Magistrate. His gentle nature and pragmatic approach to life had prompted him to stay not at Circuit House but at PWD, Dak Bungalow where I was staying in transit alongwith another Assistant Collector. We could offer him tea and biscuits only as he was to reach Jaipur early for some official meeting. My own Collector, the able and affable Mr B. Hooja arrived just in time before Mr Yati could leave for Jaipur, to pick me up for his Beawar tour. He jokingly suggested that we should keep some provisions in a fridge to cater for senior officers who dropped in occasionally like Mr Yati. The unruffled, calm 'Yati' or 'Yati Sir' was popular in the best sense with almost everyone, the high and mighty political masters, the public representatives down to Sarpanches and Panches and also among the babudom—up to Clerks and Patwaris and members of public at large while he was posted as District Officer. No one appeared to criticise him for any reason even though one might not agree with him completely. His long stint as Deputy Secretary GAD and Cabinet had made him popular for he looked after official needs of the ministers and officers with an equanimity and positive approach.

Coming in touch with him early in my career, I too looked up to him for guidance and moral support while I was posted at Barmer during 1970–1972. Thus, a few days before the polling date of Parliamentary Elections of 1971, I faced a dilemma when the then BJS party leaders insisted and formally requested me to allow the use of Government Higher Secondary School ground facing its building which also overlooked the Kotwali police station and the tri-junction of market streets. This ground had been earlier used for the Prime Minster's public address during Indira Gandhi's tour in famine time. As she was at the pinnacle of popularity in 1971 with her 'Garibi Hatao' slogan and campaign, another much larger ground located at the back of the said school was cleaned up and a new public rostrum constructed for election meeting. When I rang up to say seek guidance from 'Yati Sir' over the dilemma that BJS opposition leaders were adamant for my approval for the use of ground facing the building, he said, 'ICS (as he affectionately called me) you allot the newly done up large ground and say that in this Election, PM has used this ground and in all fairness you are allotting the same. They will come round once you tell them tactfully in your own way'. Needless to add, his advice, as DS, GAD in time came as a great relief as I could count on his support even though I handled this matter tactfully as suggested by him. Thus, opposition leaders could not counter my argument of fairness in treatment, as suggested by him. Such timely advice and guidance, I guess, was available to all those who needed it and were amenable to the idea of approaching him.

# 30

# G.K. Bhanot

## Whom We Never Forget

**B.D. Joshi**

Late Shri G.K. Bhanot was one of those rare persons whom you never forget. My first meeting with him was in the year 1975 when he was Development Commissioner in Rajasthan and I was working as Deputy Secretary, Medical and Public Health Department. One day, he just walked in my room and I was taken aback. He wanted some information regarding Medical Department, and he could have called me in his chamber but it was his greatness that he never gave importance to such trivialities and always made others feel at home. Thereafter, there were many occasions for me to meet him and my esteem and regard for him increased considerably. I used to talk about various men and matters, and he always encouraged me to give free and frank opinion about them. Sometimes, he was very much worried about falling standards of governance and increased corruption and nepotism in public life.

He was a great lover of art and literature and when he found that I also had keen interest in literature, my association with him increased further. We used to talk about various trends in the literature, specially Hindi novels and poetry.

After his retirement, besides his cultural and literary activities he took keen interest in the welfare of officers who retired from All India Services. He was patron of All India Service Officers'

(Pensioners) Association, and it was due to his efforts that various problems of the retired officers could be solved expeditiously. He attended all the meetings of the Executive Committee of the Association and its general meetings. He also took care that families of the demised officers are looked after well, and their medical problems and pension matters are well attended. Since I was Secretary of the aforesaid association, my meetings with him were frequent. He used to give detailed guidance and line of action in such matters. His habits were very simple that anybody who came in his contact never hesitated to talk to him, and he always gave free and frank opinion.

When the recommendations of Fifth Pay Commission were published, he immediately called an emergency meeting of the executive committee of the association and discussed at length, its implications on the service matters of retired officers. Thereafter, there were frequent meetings relating to these matters, and he took care that all its benefits are made available to the members of the association expeditiously. He used to phone me frequently to find out the details of the fixation cases and talked about the medical problems of the members of the association.

With his demise, state has lost not only an able administrator but also a man with great heart and wisdom. These days it is difficult to find great man like Shri Gopal Krishna Bhanot.

# 31

# S.L. Khurana

## A Man of Steel with Vision

**B.D. Joshi**

Shri S.L. Khurana was one of the best administrators I have come across. He was a good judge of persons, and once he was convinced about an officer he always relied on him. He had complete grasp over situation, and usually his judgement never went wrong.

I recollect, once there was prolonged strike of medical students, which continued for weeks. At that time, I was posted in Jaipur District Administration and he gave detailed instructions regarding handling the strike which is normally unusual at the level of Chief Secretary. His calculations regarding the strike were accurate and it fizzled out soon. During that period, there was strike of government employees also, and it had taken serious turn and grave law and orders situation had emerged. Khurana was quite firm at that time. He had complete confidence of the then Chief Minister Shri Barkatullah Khan, and there was weekly briefing to handle the strike. It was his firmness, complete grasp of the situation and faith in officers that situation never went out of control, and employees had to call off the strike unconditionally.

During his tenure as Home Secretary, I was working as Additional Director Public Relations. Though he was working as Home Secretary and public relations was a small part of the Home Department, he had full knowledge of the working of Public

Relations Department. He often gave detailed instructions regarding publication of news, organising exhibitions and release of advertisements.

He was very kind at heart and often enquired about the welfare of family members. Even if any personal problem was put before him, he used to hear it patiently and tried to help as far as possible.

His style of conducting the meeting was superb. He had complete control over agenda items and expected the same from officers attending the meeting. He never allowed the officers attending the meeting to bring their subordinates with them and expected that officers themselves should have complete grasp over the matters under consideration.

He normally shielded the officers from the political pressures and also expected that they would always act with firmness and without any fear. His elevation as Union Home Secretary proved that he was a man of steel with firm conviction and great vision.

# Part III

## The Chief Ministers

# 32

# Chief Ministers Remembered

I.C. Srivastava

Memories of interface with political leaders and powers crowd into the 'mind's eyes'. But some incidents and anecdotes can be recalled vividly, being sharply etched in memory. A great leader and Chief Minister, Rajasthan, for 17 long years, Shri M.L. Sukhadia left an indelible impression on my personality with his inimitable candour in conduct, vision of future and insight into the ground realities and need of the hour. A few months into my first assignment as Collector and District Magistrate of Barmer district early in 1971 before he resigned to make way for Shri Barkatullah Khan, Shri Sukhadia came to inaugurate Tilwara Cattle Fair near Balotra sub-divisional headquarters. After receiving him on the outskirts of the town, we escorted him to Dak Bungalow from where he proceeded directly to the fair ground. I was taken aback when he beckoned to me to come close to him immediately after alighting from the car. Looking into my eyes, he asked a simple question, 'Collector Sahib, *Aap ko mujhse alagse kuch kehna hai? Sab theek hai*'. 'Yes, Sir, everything is all right. I joined here two months back and am still studying the problems of the district'. He called the then SP Shri Dulhe Singh and asked him the same question which he had asked me, followed by another query, '*Aap dono ko kuch saath me kehna hai?*' Formalities over, he proceeded with graceful gait and joined the waiting group of Pradhan, members of Panchayat Samiti and the irrepressible lady MLA Mrs Madan Kaur. It was obvious that he was a true leader of people and knew their moods and needs too closely, free from any doubt, narrow and grooved thinking. He seated the Pradhan of Panchayat Samiti on his right side alongwith members (he knew too well how and when to keep appropriate people on the right side) and the local MLA and other leaders on his left. He addressed the gathered crowd with aplomb, grace and dignity par excellence. People nodded and responded with measured clapping. As it was the pre-election period of parliamentary elections due in March 1971 (later postponed to April 1971), Shri Sukhadia proceeded to Siwana and did not pick me up contrary to his practice to take Collector in his car for a discussion about the district's problems on way. Probably, 17 long years as CM had given him enough feedback and food for thought leaving little scope for a newly arrived officer like me to brief him further. Addressing some meetings on way, he arrived late in afternoon at Siwana and went for a brisk walk in the big courtyard behind the Dak Bungalow. After a cup of tea, he went to address the big election meeting organised on the crossing, right opposite the tehsil office and Dak Bungalow. Surprisingly, he made the Sarpanch of Siwana sit with him. Siwana, though a tehsil headquarters, had not graduated to an urban status. Here he had forgotten all about us who waited in the wings of the Dak Bungalow literally as protocol required and maintained our civil service neutrality from a safe distance.

Shri Sukhadia's grace and greatness blended well with his essential humility when he came to visit Barmer in the month following his resignation as CM, in a black party car without the grandiose of security and frills of power. He was required to supervise civil defence arrangements alongwith Shri M.D. Mathur, his erstwhile Finance Minister who was declared Secretary General, Civil Defence Council, Government of India. Needless to add, his visit boosted the morale of the people before the impending war, which loomed large on the horizon. However, he was all humility when we went to call on him at the Dak Bungalow. He was visibly pleased as we had gone to see him on our own out of sheer courtesy without any hint or call from him or his local followers and party cadre.

A tall leader and a great personae who overshadowed all state leaders for a long time richly deserves a sharply etched, unique niche in the history of Rajasthan for his visionary zeal and astute management of politics. His famous smile and cool composure helped him win over multitudes of common people who reposed full faith in his stewardship of the state's affairs. The industrialisation of the state received a great fillip during his tenure besides all round development under a stable government. Kota was declared the first industrial town of the state which slowly and steadily also developed as a tourist destination under his able leadership.

Another Congress leader with whom I came in contact stands out as great political stalwart. If one goes by the adage, some are born great, some achieve greatness and some others have greatness thrust upon them. While Shri Sukhadia was a great achiever, Shri Barkatullah Khan had the greatness thrust upon him. He was called upon by the then Prime Minister Indira Gandhi to assume the mantle of Chief Ministership immediately on his return from a visit to Middle East when Shri Sukhadia was asked to step down ostensibly for his supporting Congress (O) leaders, Morarji Desai and others who had split the Congress Party.

Shri Barkatullah Khan with his buxom demeanour and heavy gait gave the impression of an easy-going person but on a close contact he revealed the essential human and humane side of his personality. The imminent war with Pakistan arising from India's intervention in the ongoing war between Mukti Bahini of the erstwhile East Pakistan and Pakistan army provided opportunities to me as Collector, Barmer to come in contact directly with Shri Khan. His bear hug on alighting from the plane at Uttarlai or car besides generating warmth also kindled the right mood and spirit for interaction with him individually or during meeting with officers. An occasional pat on the shoulder was also in order to serve the same purpose. This warmth in relationship was clearly reflected in the following two episodes. In the last week of October 1971, an officers' meeting was convened in the Dak Bungalow under the chairmanship of Chief Minister to review and gear up the preparatory measures for the war, which was considered a certainty in view of the assistance provided by Indian forces to Mukti Bahini. Just before the start of the meeting, sitting beside the Chief Minister, at the head of the table, hesitatingly I opened the ordinary non-official envelope containing the letter from my wife who had delivered a son on 15 September 1971. Before I could glance through the contents, the CM happened to notice the letter and asked me in whispers 'Is it from your wife? Go ahead and read it'. My gestures revealed all and in sheer excitement I told him in low tone and voice, 'My wife wants to join me here urgently but I wish to tell her not to come over here due to imminent war as the child is barely a month and half'. God only knows what inner voice prompted Shri Khan to exclaim, 'You know, Gentlemen, Collector Sahib's wife wants to join him in his war effort alongwith a small child and Srivastavaji is going to tell her not to come to Barmer. I think Collector's wife is more brave. I am asking him here not to prevent her from coming here as it will give a good boost to the morale of the officers' families and to others as well'. I was flabbergasted and speechless for a while and then everyone had a hearty laugh as I gave a nod in agreement with CM's suggestion which left no scope for any further thinking. I telephoned Archana to come post-haste as the clouds of war were gathering and threatening to burst before long. Needless to add, her arrival not only set the house in order but also raised the spirits of the members of officers' families living in the government colony located behind the Collector's bungalow.

The other episode relates to the aftermath of the bombing of railway station of Barmer on the night of 8th–9th December 1971 by Pakistani fighter planes. CM was visiting Jaisalmer on the 9th December and was scheduled to come to Barmer on the 10th December. Shri Bhim Singh, the then Border Commissioner discussed the situation in the wake of bombing as aforesaid. After I explained to him at some length, the situation especially the departure of some traders' families in panic and also about the efforts we were making to keep up the sagging morale of the people by addressing them on the microphone network address system and by convening Citizens' Council meeting, Shri Bhim Singh—a highly experienced but a flamboyant officer—initially did not agree with my advice to CM (to be conveyed through him) to postpone his visit to Barmer on 10th December 1971 as scheduled, by a few days so that we could bring the situation under control especially by making urgent and earnest request to Air Commodore at Jodhpur to provide night cover to Barmer town by deploying MIGs at Uttarlai. When the arrival of MIGs was announced by a loud bang of their crossing the sound barrier, people sighed with great relief. Shri Bhim Singh telephoned again to say that CM had expressed a desire to come despite my advice. With complete composure and in a clear tone, I insisted that my advice, given on grounds of security, should be accepted. The Chief Minister graciously relented and decided not to come for a few more days. When CM did come later, after his usual affectionate bear hug, he gave me a pat on the back for handling the situation well.

I must also pay tribute to Shri B.S. Shekhawat, another towering political personality and leader of Rajasthan, considered and acclaimed as next only to Shri M.L. Sukhadia in political acumen, sagacity and wisdom gained by his long innings in politics of the state. He was elected Chief Minister three times but completed only one full spell of five years from 1993 to 1998. As I can recall, my first face-to-face meeting with Shri Bhairon Singhji (as he was normally addressed) took place when I called on him after my posting as Collector, Bharatpur, in July 1977. I was rather on the horns of a dilemma (having faced three transfers since August 1976) whether to go to Bharatpur or remain at Jaipur by making a request to CM directly. A warm hand on the shoulder and a pat on my back by Shri Shekhawat overwhelmed me, and I could not utter anything when he said, '*Mere kahne se chalejaiye*'. A revolutionary change in government on 'Janata Party' wave had brought him to power and position of Chief Ministership for the first time and the whiff of rising expectations of people also filled me with a new zeal to work in my 'old' district which was already familiar to me, having worked as Sub-divisional Officer (headquarters) at Bharatpur for more than two years. Probably, Shri Shekhawat was quite confident that I would be able to face floods and provide relief to people with my earlier experience because he visited Bharatpur the same day but left before my arrival in the evening by the last train which I had taken to travel with family for taking charge there in the midst of swirling flood waters. Surrounded by floods on the outskirts on almost all sides, Bharatpur people were facing 'deluge', so to say, and I, therefore, plunged myself into my duties and rounds of the city without taking formal charge after being briefed by the officers for about half an hour.

After about 10 months, Shri Shekhawat, however, had to transfer me, reportedly under great pressure from his erstwhile Emergency Jail co-inmate of Bharatpur, who wanted to play favour based 'transfer' politics with me. But with my reputation and earlier stint in their mind, they knew that he could not get Patwaris and ILRs transferred by making polite requests to me or even on the basis of complaints unless I was satisfied about the genuineness of requests or complaints. That 'transfer is no punishment' is an oft-cited adage in government, conveniently cited to suit the convenience of the person and the occasion. Thus, I had to undergo 27 transfers in 37 years of my career in the IAS. But I was never disheartened with the 'strange but true' ways of government. However, the then Chief Secretary' Shri Bhanot was courteous and gracious enough to have called me to Jaipur to explain the background. He almost apologetically asked me to go for next posting as Excise Commissioner at Udaipur where my brothers and parents were also living, a fact which was also cited by him additionally to smooth my ruffled feelings.

However, Shri Shekhawat never lost the confidence he had reposed in me and time and again it showed in the course of my working relationship with him during his second and third spells as Chief Minister. I was posted as Secretary, Education, Irrigation, CAD, Food and Civil Supplies and Revenue, by him and finally as Chairman, Board of Revenue, Ajmer, in September 1998 before the Assembly elections in November in which BJP was defeated. He did give me some advice not only in a friendly manner but also as an elderly leader. Once he remarked, '*Srivastavaji, aap seedhe hee yes-no kar dete hain, hamare liye kuch kahne ko rahne dijiye. Kuch kagaj, kuch samay rakhiye. Jaldi mein jawab mat dijiye*'. As Principal Secretary,

Revenue, I had told a delegation of representatives, mostly Sarpanches, that Karauli during that year would not be notified as a district for various reasons, although Kumat Committee set up to examine this matter had given a favourable recommendation in this regard. They, then, approached CM, who could not contradict me in their presence nor could he give any definite answer. Hence, his above-mentioned friendly advice.

Shri Shekhawat was a self-made leader. He had imbibed some leadership qualities of Shri M.L. Sukhadia who was reportedly his 'mentor' in private and opponent in public, being leaders of rival political parties. Humility, wit, patience, perseverance and persuasive skills were hallmark of his personality, which reflected his qualities in all places and on all occasions. An incident affecting my promotion and career would illustrate it better. As I had enjoyed his confidence, there was no reason to think otherwise despite some of my transfers necessitated by exigencies of situations, political or otherwise. But when I was promoted in the grade of Principal Secretary and posted in January 1994 as Chairman, Rajasthan Tax Tribunal at Ajmer, I lost my patience and called on him to represent that both my daughter and son were studying in the final year of MA and engineering courses respectively and I could not shift my family to Ajmer for obvious reasons. He was all courtesy and with great humility and grace, said, '*Mujhse galti ho gayee. Mujhe dhyan nahin tha. Main aaj, aur abhi aapke Jaipur posting ke order kar detah hoon*'. On my further submission and query whether I had committed any mistake and was, therefore, no longer in his good books, his forthright reply was, '*Aap ki nishtha, karya kshmta aur mehnat ke bare mein mujhe kabhi sandeh nahin raha*'. The same day orders posting me as Principal Secretary, Revenue, Colonisation and Devasthan, were issued. I remained in that position for more than three years and this gave me great satisfaction in formulating two sets of new draft legislation namely the Rajasthan Tenancy Bill 1996 and Rajasthan Land Revenue Bill 1996. Drafted in consultation with a legislative committee headed by Revenue Minister himself, both the bills were introduced in the State Assembly with delay and thus could not be passed as the general elections were looming large on the horizon in

1998 and no political party was willing to put its stakes on the passing of these bills.

To my mind, Shri Shekhawat will go down in history as a great visionary leader who indefatigably worked for an all round development of the state with an emphasis on education and empowerment of women, which received a great fillip during his Chief Ministership. He proved to be a tall stalwart in the national and regional politics. Finally, he showed his sharp mettle and deep political wisdom in steering, for five years, the proceedings of Rajya Sabha as Chairman and Vice President of India. He has rightly earned a unique niche for himself in national history and politics.

# 33

# Chief Ministers

## Rare Glimpses

**P.N. Bhandari**

I had the proud privilege of serving directly or indirectly under several Chief Ministers. Shri Mohan Lal Sukhadia was the longest serving Chief Minister of Rajasthan. Due to several postings of mine in Udaipur, I came in close contact with him. He was a man of the masses—totally accessible to the people at large. Every morning while taking a stroll in Durga Nursery (his farmhouse in the heart of Udaipur city), he would meet a large number of people. He was ever smiling. He was truly a great statesman and had a very good rapport even with the leaders in the opposition.

As a Commercial Taxes Officer, I attached a few buses of one of the close relatives of Shri Sukhadia, in view of the heavy arrears of passengers and goods tax. This audacious action was like a storm in the tea cup and had jolted the higher circles both in Udaipur and Jaipur. Shri Mathura Das Mathur, the then Finance Minister, telephoned me and cautioned that such a step would embarrass the Chief Minister while the Vidhan Sabha was in session and he (FM) may be misunderstood by the Chief Minister. I, however, evaded the pressure and was able to recover heavy arrears. In another case, I attached the bank account of a liquor baron of Udaipur due to huge arrears of sales tax. He too was highly connected. The Commissioner, Commercial Taxes, Shri N.C. Bhatnagar who also belonged to Udaipur, called me and remarked, 'You have perhaps prepared a list of all those who are in the inner circle of the Chief Minister and you are specially pressurizing them for recovery'. I explained to him that it was just accidental but obviously, our Assistant Commercial Taxes Officers and Inspectors had made good recoveries in most of the cases. They, however, did not dare to touch the influential persons. Hence, I had to focus on the dues against such VIPs. In spite of these acts of omission and commission by me as a very junior officer, Shri Sukhadia never tried to harm me even remotely.

I recall another incident. Shri Sukhadia was Governor of Karnataka. Some RAS officer had come to me late in the night. His brother was seriously ill and needed urgent attention in Bangalore. He wanted me to telephone Shri Sukhadia in Bangalore. Being a very junior officer, I could not muster courage to telephone Shri Sukhadia but when the officer persisted, I attempted a phone call around 10.30 p.m. To my utter surprise, Shri Sukhadia himself lifted the phone and made prompt arrangements for the patient. I was deeply touched by the human touch behind his response. In the normal course, even middle-ranking officers do not easily come on phone. I recall, as Collector, once due to some urgent work I telephoned the Chief Secretary at about 7.30 in the morning. The Chief Secretary was annoyed that I had unnecessarily woken him so early the morning.

I had also served in various capacities under Shri Hari Deo Joshi while he was Chief Minister. He rarely smiled. He was a man of few words. He was very decisive, and his time management was remarkable. He would never waver and decide matters in minutes. Once he had called me and Shri M.D. Kaurani, Commissioner, JDA, for some discussions. Shri Kaurani was about to occupy the chair when Shri Joshi conveyed his decision and the meeting was over. He avoided micromanagement. He would convey his views in the briefest possible way. Very often, after returning from a meeting with him, we would ponder over the signals behind his telegraphic directions. As Secretary, Urban Development and LSG, I had started for the first time, the outsourcing of garbage removal through private contractors for Jaipur Municipal Corporation. The Safai Karmacharis protested and went on strike. Elections were in the offing. No politician would risk his votes however commendable the scheme may be. I was sceptical that the CM may yield to pressure, but Shri Joshi did not waver and firmly stood by the decision. Finally the strike was called off, and the outsourcing arrangements got stabilised.

As Commissioner, Commercial Taxes, I once took a list of proposed transfers of Commercial Taxes officers as Shri Joshi also held the finance portfolio. Without even looking at the names, he approved the list. After signing, he observed that the transfer list was very long. I explained to him that many of the transfers were on request and hence no travelling allowance was to be paid. The matter ended at that. Nowadays, when even the transfers of peons are done at the level of Cabinet Ministers, one may not believe that the transfer list of the officers of the biggest revenue-earning department would be signed by the Chief Minister/FM in less than 1 minute without even a single change. Such was the level of Shri Joshi's faith in senior officers. The present generation of officers may not believe that the transfer proposals could be finalised without the dossier of 'desires' of MLAs and others.

During the Emergency, I was Collector, Udaipur. I had launched a big encroachment removal drive in Udaipur. While the public at large supported the drive, some vested interests were annoyed. To add fuel to fire, the projected *Chabutri* of Congress office was also demolished in the road-widening campaign. Some people complained to the Chief Minister and he was furious. He took me and our SP Shri Ram Narayan in his car and on the way conveyed his extreme displeasure. He said, 'People feel that my orders may not be carried out but your orders are implemented in hot haste'. I muttered something in defence but there was hardly any scope for a detailed explanation before him. The concerned group was elated at the development and soon their delegation called on the Chief Minister in Jaipur requesting for my transfer. They were, however, rudely shaken when the Chief Minister flatly refused telling them that he too had to show his performance at the national level to the Prime Minister Mrs Indira Gandhi. 'Udaipur and Alwar districts were showing the best performance in 20-point programme and I cannot afford to disturb these Collectors'. Shri Adarsh Kishore Saxena was Collector, Alwar at that time.

I had served earlier as Vice Chancellor, and later as Commissioner, Commercial Taxes, during the Chief Ministership of Shri Shiv Charan Mathur. He was fond of recording lengthy notes on the files. He was very articulate in both Hindi and English. He was greatly impressed with my work in the Commercial Taxes Department. Usually, the meeting of Budget Finalisation Committee (BFC) in the Finance Department is taken by some Deputy Secretary of FD. To convey his strong support to our department, Shri Mathur once told me that he would like to take the BFC meeting of our department.

As Vice Chancellor, Udaipur, there were certain very sensitive problems. The Governor, Air Chief Marshal Mehra, was greatly impressed with my work but he was equally displeased with my outspoken and independent style. In the armed forces, there is no scope for dissent and a senior officer will expect nothing but 'Yes Sir', from the officers down below. I did not fit in that category; hence, the Governor was personally annoyed with me. He ordered for a Search Committee for filling up the post of Vice Chancellor under the Chairmanship of Justice P.N. Bhagwati, the then sitting judge of the Supreme Court. In his communication to Justice Bhagwati, with endorsement to me, the Governor mentioned that the Udaipur University was repeatedly delaying the finalisation of the name of its representative for the Search Committee.

I wrote to Hon'ble Justice Bhagwati, mentioning that my appointment was for the residuary period and hence any question of Search Committee was totally premature. I also faintly hinted that in view of the legal complications, if a lower court were to grant stay order against the Search Committee meeting, it would be embarrassing for an eminent judge of the Apex Court. I also reminded him that without resorting to such circuitous measures, I could be simply transferred by the state government to another post. In spite of this sustained and relentless pressure by the Governor, Shri Shiv Charan Mathur as Chief Minister did not yield and stood like a rock behind me. He was mighty glad with the all-round improvement in the working of the University during my tenure. Today, when MLAs are able to engineer transfer of officials on the slightest provocation, it is difficult to imagine that even the Governor's pressure for transfer would not work.

I recall another incident. Shri Mathur was a Cabinet Minister at that time. In a state-level conference, I had mooted some scheme. At the end of my presentation, he observed, 'I have not understood your scheme but I have seen your past performance, so go ahead with your scheme'. Such was the level of personal confidence of Shri Mathur once he was familiar with the working of an officer.

In spite of his personal views on certain matters, he was flexible enough and was equally receptive to the contrary views also. I recall participating in one of his cabinet meetings. The issue was how much development cost to be charged from the developers of the various housing societies. Shri Mathur was strongly of the view that all developers should not be put at par. While some developers had invested substantial funds for the development of infrastructure, others had done very little. As Secretary, Urban Development, I was arguing against any subjective decision on this issue. I argued that the JDA had no record of the expenses incurred by the developers in the various housing colonies. Those who had incurred substantial expenditure in the development of roads, etc., they were able to get higher prices for the sale of their plots while others who had not done anything substantial, their earning was also limited from those areas. After a lot of debate on this issue, one senior officer sent Shri M.D. Korani, JDC, from behind to whisper in my ears that perhaps the CM is impressed by the very good Infrastructure developed by the Housing Society in Shyam Nagar where he had built his own house. In spite of this feedback, I stuck to my stand and the CM was provoked to say that I was 'bull-dozing' the cabinet on this issue. I pleaded that there was no such intention but I said that as Secretary to the Government I would be failing in my duty to my masters if I did not correctly advise them. Finally, the CM gave up his idea of having differential rates of development charges from the housing societies. Such instances of democratic approach are rare, where a CM would be willing to give up his pet idea at the instance of an officer. I must also say that even after that incident Shri Mathur at no stage displayed any displeasure towards me—rather his faith and confidence in me had gone up.

Under the Chief Ministership of Shri Bhairon Singh Shekhawat also, I had served in various capacities. He was very witty and in his presence there was no tension. With his disarming charm, he would put you at ease. He had an elephantine memory and would meticulously keep record of old events and happenings. He too was a man of masses and had picked up many qualities from Shri Mohan Lal Sukhadia. I found that Shri Shekhawat had excellent relations even with the Leader of the Opposition. Notwithstanding the fiery debates in the Vidhan Sabha, there was no trace of any hostility or bitterness in their personal interaction. He was easily accessible to the people and the officers. Through his official and private sources, he was very well informed about the working of officers and even their private activities.

Shri Shekhawat contested MLAs election from Chhabra in Kota district. I was Collector in that district. The Congress party had challenged his nomination papers before our SDO who was the Returning Officer. They argued that being a Rajya Sabha Member from Madhya Pradesh, his name was registered in MP and hence it could not be included in the voter list of Rajasthan. After watching the developments, I reported to the CM who was camping at Chhabra that the matter was getting complicated and the objections raised by the Congress party were weighty and could not be easily brushed aside. Shri Shekhawat, however, stoically observed that he was advised that there is no legal problem but he will abide by the decision of the Returning Officer. I can never forget his philosophic resignation to destiny on such a crucial issue which threatened his Chief Ministership itself. If any other Minister or Chief Minister was in his place, he would have pressed that by hook or crook his nomination papers must be accepted.

As Commissioner, Commercial Taxes, I had exercised perhaps for the first time the Commissioner's power for waiver, of old arrears. Basically my strategy was to recover old dues, which had become virtually irrecoverable for years together. Broadly I was tempting the assessees to pay the principal amount if they wanted waiver of substantial interest. One of the senior BJP MLAs in the opposition complained in the Vidhan Sabha about the misuse of that power by me. As Leader of the Opposition, Shri Shekhawat rose to contradict his Party's MLA and defended me. In fact, MLAs from both the Ruling Party and Opposition supported me. Later in a function, I happened to meet Shri Shekhawat. I profusely thanked him particularly because he chose to contradict his own Party's MLA. Shri Shekhawat replied in his inimitable style. He said, 'By levelling allegations against hard honest officers like you, our credibility suffers'. Once Shri Shekhawat was convinced about the credentials of an officer, he would give him a free hand and full support. His insight about the capacity of officers was phenomenal and he always tried to put the right person at the right job.

Shri Shekhawat was democratic to the core and never displayed any authoritarian touch in his working as Chief Minister. Even while transferring he often sounded me in advance. At one stage, when a student had committed suicide, and there were large-scale disturbances in the Rajasthan University, he summoned me to accept the Vice Chancellorship. Years ago, I had been Vice Chancellor of Udaipur University, and he was conscious of my performance there. I, however, politely declined the offer and he respected my refusal. He once jocularly told me, 'You have built up such a high reputation that even if you were to tell total lies, people would still believe your version'.

When I was in RSEB, he once told me to take a class of ministers. I pleaded that it would be against protocol. Finally, it was decided that I would make an exclusive presentation before the Cabinet about RSEB. It was a very lively session. One of the Cabinet Ministers even walked out saying that he could not win an argument with me.

He once told me that many people in his constituency (Chhabra) were not happy with the public dealing of the SDO, Shri J.L. Modi. I, however, defended the SDO for his honesty and uprightness. The CM went by my advice and closed the matter. How many CMs would accept such advice in their own constituency?

Ms Amarjit Kaur was my SDO in Udaipur District. When I was Collector, Kota, she was posted as Collector, Bundi. She was a very tough officer. Some MLA had written to her for the transfer of a Patwari in his constituency. She charge-sheeted the Patwari for bringing political influence in service matters. The matter came to CM's notice. Next time, when he visited Kota, on his return trip, he took me to Bundi to advise the Collector that she might, if necessary, charge-sheet the Patwari but she should avoid dragging the name of the MLA in the charge sheet. As CM, he could have directly spoken to the Collector but such was his grace that he preferred my advising to her rather than his directly telling her.

## A Faith Fortified

In nutshell, time and again, my faith has been fortified that administration can be made more responsive the tendency to function thoughtlessly and indifferently can be curbed in the new context, rules and procedures can be given a fresh look, and precedence can be given to logic and reasoning instead of outdated rules. Administration should focus on major issues rather than getting bogged down in trivialities, with the active help of the public and public representatives, a new and a forward push can be given to the various development schemes and the stigma of red-tape can be removed with simplification of rules and procedures.

# Contributors

**J.S. Mehta,** former Education Commissioner and Secretary to the Government of Rajasthan, Relief and Rehabilitation. He had also been Chief Commissioner Scouts Rajasthan. In his leadership, scout movement reached great heights in Rajasthan.

**Pradyumna Kumar,** former Collector and District Magistrate Jhunjhunu and Jhalawar. He is the Managing Trustee of Krishna Gopal Ayurvedic Bhawan Charitable Trust and is also associated with various social activities.

**V.B.L. Mathur,** former Chief Secretary, Government of Rajasthan and Adviser to Governor. A man of vision with great administrative ability and acumen.

**Sudhindra Gemawat,** formerly Collector and District Magistrate Sikar and Managing Director, Scheduled Castes and Scheduled Tribes Development Corporation. He has written several books and is presently associated with various social organisations.

**V.D. Sharma** was an eminent administrator and a literary figure. He retired as Home Secretary, Government of Rajasthan, and thereafter Member of Rajasthan Public Service Commission and Chairman, Rajasthan Sahitya Academy.

**I.C. Srivastava,** former Chairman, Board of Revenue and Chairman, Rajasthan Mines and Minerals Limited. He has authored several books and is associated with various social activities. He is also President, Transparency International, Rajasthan Chapter.

**P.K.B. Kurup,** former Chairman, HCM Rajasthan State Institute of Public Administration and Chairman, Rajasthan Civil Services Appellate Tribunal. He had been associated with various social activities.

**Mohan Mukerji,** former Chief Secretary, Government of Rajasthan and Adviser to Governor. He had also served as Additional Secretary, Culture in the Ministry of Education, Government of India. He took keen interest in academic and cultural activities and has written several books.

**Krishna Bhatnagar,** former Senior Adviser Planning Commission, Joint Secretary and Financial Adviser, Department of Agriculture Research, Government of India, New Delhi. She was Collector and District Magistrate, Ajmer, and also held several important posts in the State Administration.

**R.S. Kumat,** former Chairman, Board of Revenue and Secretary Education, Government of Rajasthan. He had done excellent work in the field of Scouting and Adult Education. Presently, he is associated with various social organisations.

**I.S. Kavadia,** former Chairman, Board of Revenue, Director, HCM Rajasthan State Institute of Public Administration and Chairman, Rajasthan State Road Transport Corporation. He also served as CMD, Jaipur Metals and Electricals Limited.

**Abhimanyu Singh,** former Education Secretary, Government of Rajasthan. He also served as Collector and District Magistrate, Tonk and Alwar. After seeking voluntary retirement from the IAS, he also worked in UNESCO headquarters at Paris.

**M.L. Mehta,** former Chief Secretary, Government of Rajasthan and Additional Secretary (Home), Government of India, and Director, HCM Institute of Public Administration. He takes keen interest in various social activities.

**Rajendra Bhanawat** is the Managing Director, Rajasthan Industrial and Investment Corporation. He has worked as Collector of various districts and also served as Commissioner, Bharatpur Division.

**B.D. Joshi,** former Chairman, Rajasthan State Text Book Board and Special Secretary (Education), Government of Rajasthan. Besides, he also served as Collector and District Magistrate in various districts. He has written several books which cover health and social aspects.

**Jagat Pal Singh** served as Collector and District Magistrate, Churu, and also held other important posts in state administration. He has served as Secretary, Indian Institute of Crafts and Designs from 1 March 1995 to 31 December 2003 after his superannuation. Presently, he is busy with the writing of a book *Pilgrimage of Solar Deities in Rajasthan.*

**P.N. Bhandari,** former Additional Chief Secretary, Rajasthan, Chairman, Rajasthan State Electricity Board and Chairman, Rajasthan Industrial and Investment Corporation. He has also worked as Collector and District Magistrate in various districts. He is remembered as one of the most innovative civil servants.